THE BETRAYAL
OF GOD

LITERARY CURRENTS IN BIBLICAL INTERPRETATION

THE
BETRAYAL
OF
GOD

---

ideological
conflict
in
job

DAVID PENCHANSKY

Westminster/John Knox Press
Louisville, Kentucky

THE BETRAYAL OF GOD: IDEOLOGICAL CONFLICT IN JOB

© 1990 David Penchansky

First edition

Published by Westminster/John Knox Press
Louisville, Kentucky

PRINTED IN THE UNITED STATES OF AMERICA
2 4 6 8 9 7 5 3 1

Library of Congress Cataloging-in-Publication Data

Penchansky, David.
  The betrayal of God : ideological conflict in Job / David Penchansky.
— 1st ed.
      p.   cm. — (Literary currents in biblical interpretation)
  Includes bibliographical references and indexes.
  ISBN 0-664-25123-4

  1. Bible. O.T. Job—Criticism, interpretation, etc. 2. Bible. O.T. Job
—Criticism, Textual. I. Title. II. Series.
BS1415.2.P44 1990
223′.1066—dc20   90-38429

What's that beside how God betrays this bleeding world for sport each bleeding bloody day? Hell and his fires has no crueler torments than the way he buggers us that serves him best. What's friends and gentleness to him? What's broken hearts? What Hell is worse than life itself?

— Frederick Buechner
  Brendan

CONTENTS

SERIES
PREFACE

New currents in biblical interpretation are emerging. Questions about origins—authors, intentions, settings—and stages of composition are giving way to questions about the literary qualities of the Bible, the play of its language, the coherence of its final form, and the relations between text and readers.

Such literary criticism is rapidly acquiring sophistication as it learns from major developments in secular critical theory, especially in understanding the instability of language and the key role of readers in the production of meaning. Biblical critics are being called to recognize that a plurality of readings is an inevitable and legitimate consequence of the interpretive process. By the same token, interpreters are being challenged to take responsibility for the theological, social, and ethical implications of their readings.

Biblical interpretation is changing on the practical as well as the theoretical level. More readers, both inside and outside the academic guild, are discovering that the Bible in literary perspective can powerfully engage people's lives. Communities of faith where the Bible is foundational may find that literary criticism can make the Scripture accessible in a way that historical criticism seems unable to do.

Within these changes lie exciting opportunities for all who seek contemporary meaning in the ancient texts. The goal of the series is to encourage such change and such search, to breach the confines of traditional biblical criticism, and to open channels for new currents of interpretation.

—THE EDITORS

PREFACE

My son Simon, then three years old, said to me in a conversation, "God is a naughty little girl." I am indebted to him for that thought, and because he was always a presence in my writing of this book.

Those familiar with current trends in biblical criticism will recognize immediately my debt to James Crenshaw of Duke University. I am proud to call him friend as well as mentor/teacher.

But the book is dedicated to Joyce, and deservedly so. Her encouragement and her comments and suggestions were most needed and appreciated more than she will ever realize.

—DAVID PENCHANSKY

1

THE
DISPARATE
TEXT

INTRODUCTION

Conflicting voices in the book of Job clamor to be heard. Most readings of Job are deficient because they attempt to harmonize, compelling the book to say only one thing. Job embodies a powerful example of the disparate text, an act of literature that is characteristically unstable, a place of conflict. Elements of Job come from different genres; and the juxtaposition of parts produces obvious seams and gaping fissures in the text, in style, in characterization, and in theological concern.

How does one confront a disparate text? Many interpreters tune out all of the voices except one, and read only that voice. One might take a structure (formal characteristics) or a theme (the surface features) and compel the text to agree with that reading. Discoveries would be made, but Job's tangle of complexities would be ignored.

Often, the goal of interpretation has been to stabilize a text by making it conform to an ideological point of view, which is usually the interpreter's view of reality. However, such attempts at harmonization inevitably do violence to the text. Too much input comes from the reader's harmonious picture of the world, and is external to the written work, so that the reader discovers only his or her own reflection. A more adequate approach would presume that there are some texts that resist any attempt at harmonization.

Most literary criticism supports the view of the world held by the powerful, and, in turn, this view or ideology[1] dramatically reduces the critic's interpretive options. As a result of this ideological interference, the critic often misconstrues the text altogether. It is common, for example, to read Job as a sermon on steadfastness; hence, a prevalent view of the book throughout its critical history is of "the patience of Job." Such ideological construals of texts are inescapable for the interpreter.[2] However, the reader might at least widen his or her ideological horizon, by reflecting upon the reading and those aspects of the text that resist it. The reader can thereby begin to examine his or her community of interpretation (the shared ideological construct), and see things from a different perspective. In so doing, the reader can highlight key features of the text often overlooked.

APPROACHES TO DISSONANCE

Only those reading strategies that engage in "metacommentary[3]" (reflection upon the processes of interpretation itself) will be at all sensitive to the disparate text. One must first be suspicious of one's own method, or at least reflective upon the tensions created by the method, before the cracks and gaps in the text begin to appear. I define dissonance using the metaphor of sound, as the effect produced by two or more clashing elements that cannot be resolved in harmony. Few critics have made dissonance their point of study, examining the gaps between the meanings of texts.[4] Those who do, Pierre Macherey (1978) and Fredric Jameson (1971, 1972, 1982) in particular, will provide a philosophical and methodological framework to examine the disparate features in the text of Job.[5] These critics must, however, be contextualized, placed in their intellectual setting. I shall proceed therefore to examine how formalism (refering to the generally inclusive movement which asserts that the form of the text is of chief importance), Marxism, and Deconstruction contributed to the intellectual development of Jameson and Macherey.

10

Formalism

The idea of human perfectibility through science ruled much of European intellectual history through the nineteenth and early twentieth century. Scholars from many fields used scientific paradigms in their work. Unchanging truth, it was believed, could be objectively discerned through scientific methods. This scientism or historicism prevailed in most of Europe, but movements most notably in France, the Soviet Union and the United States arose which utterly rejected this nineteenth century scientific model.

The elusive term "Structuralism," a particular expression of Formalism, has been employed to convey a wide spectrum of ideas. Structuralism usually refers to the primarily French movement asserting linguistics as the general model for human communication, including literature, and Russian Formalism is a Soviet movement with similar sensibilities. Different cultures and different disciplines have produced different manifestations of Structuralism. There are, however, family resemblances due to cross-pollination of intellectual movements and similar political situations in the intellectual community and the larger societal context.

In France, Structuralism fought against the scientific naturalism so prevalent in the literature of the time, rejecting an excessively content-oriented literary discussion. French Structuralism maintained that the essential meanings of texts were to be found in their structure,[6] the static, unchanging forms in which various particular discourses took shape. This structure was identified by the juxtaposition of repeating patterns of texts and words, or by repeated mythic forms found in all human texts, which reflect patterns in the brain. Structure also refers to the rises and falls of the narrative or dramatic movement, with comic and tragic shapes being discerned in the work. In each case, the search for structure centers on hidden values and patterns not readily apparent, rather than on what has been traditionally called "the content."

In the Soviet Union, where Socialist Realism was acknowledged as the only valid art form, the loosely organized movement known as Russian Formalism dissented. This movement insisted that literature did not represent the social conditions in society accurately and without distortion, that its purpose was not necessarily to reveal social ills and project an idealized society. Rather, the text was dramatically distinct from the external world that produced it, and reflected the forms which emanated from the deepest fabric that constituted the human community. These forms are rendered meaningful through the process of "defamiliarization" (Jameson 1972:75-79), whereby literature places the old forms in a jarring context, thus freshening them. This use of language breaks down reified symbols, revitalizing and expanding the interpretational boundaries.

Stalinist authorities ruthlessly suppressed Russian Formalists, as this group (although mostly dedicated Marxists) threatened the Soviet sense of homogeneity with a healthy dose of pluralism. The critics' view of history opposed the accepted party line, and so the Russian Formalists were thrown in prison and executed. As a result, Western critics remained unaware of their writings until fairly recently. Structuralism, although little understood, has made an impact in most disciplines and in much creative endeavor produced in the second half of the twentieth century.[7]

Formalistic approaches (including Structuralism) agree that the object of study is the text itself, apart from the world. Literature exists in its own world and runs by its own rules. No longer can one approach the task of literary criticism by seeking to isolate and examine the world to which the texts refer, the signified. Rather, one examines the text itself on its own terms.

Most formalist schools reject an historical approach to literature, asserting instead that meaning resides not in an explanation of a text's influences and origins, but rather in a text's underside, hidden from immediate purview. This rejection of history profoundly influenced later schools of criticism, with its enduring ideas finding a place in new systems. Some of its controversial assertions provide a point of departure when rejected by the new approaches. There are, within Structuralism and Russian Formalism, pronouncements which they hold in common, perhaps due to the similar nature of their antagonists and the particular unified intellectual world they both confronted:

1) Language separates into a changeable surface and an unchanging structure, a structure intimately linked with the very fabric of oral and written communication.

2) Formalism embodies a search for those aspects of literature that are universal and harmonious—corresponding to the underlying structures. Empirical criticism claimed that literature accurately reflects non-textual reality without any distortion or interpretation. Written communications have a single point. They are "about" something. The form could be discarded and the true essence of the story would remain: a propositional statement, the kernel of meaning. Formalism, however, points to the wrappings or husks; the containers of the text that are the true sources of meaning. This shift in emphasis expands the possibilities of interpretation. These "husks" often speak in opposition to the traditional idea of "content." Two narratives or poems placed in proximity might thereby comment powerfully on each other. When one reads the two pieces "anthologically," that is, as part of a collection, new voices speak, contradicting or offering alternatives to the original readings.

3) These structures often conflict with the surface content.[8] The underlying form most profoundly communicates the factors that contribute to the production of a literary work. Contents conceal the operations of literature. The form embodies the very shape of the narrative: the juxtaposition of information as well as repeated patterns which have often been identified with structural studies. Because juxtaposition is largely an unconscious process, it reflects subliminal efforts of an interest group to manipulate and control the structures of society.

4) Nineteenth century criticism was dominated by an empiricism which searched for external historical causes for the literary effects. Features of the text were therefore isolated from the whole and displayed like butterflies on a pinning board. This approach left its stamp upon many subsequent critical approaches. Formalism opposes this view by insisting that the external world contributes little to an understanding of the literary text. Formalism stresses the relationships that take place

within a text. Meaning (Formalists say) is generated only in the textual arena.[9] Writing therefore is iceberg-thick; all that has not been said lurks under the surface. Our attention is focused on the gaps, the most important aspects of the written material,[10] the things the text does not say, what it avoids and hides, and which become apparent only through an examination of structure.[11]

Claude Lévi-Strauss, a Structuralist working in the field of anthropology, observes that myths function in society to cover up or conceal absences, gaps, and internal contradictions which run as fault-lines throughout the superstructure (1976: 203-204).[12] Jameson widens the application of this insight by affirming that ideological conflict would necessarily be concealed in the production and dissemination of all texts (1981: 77-80), not myths exclusively. The act of concealment itself must be a subject of careful scrutiny, for it can be a key to the meaning of the work.

This picture of formalist movements must be contextualized in history. By noting the determined character of structuralism, certain blind spots and weaknesses emerge.

Structuralism and Russian Formalism shared with their adversaries the view that the essence of literature was found in certain unchanging verities discoverable through proper scientific technique. They merely saw these verities as resident in different places. Later critical approaches, although influenced by the formalist view that the center of literature is hidden, dissented from the formalist avoidance of history. These formalist flaws become pronounced as an ever more violent history impinged upon literary consciousness.

Formalism as an entire system then, does not adequately understand the phenomenon of dissonance. Literature, it claims, makes sense when examined structurally. Formalism offers a description of something timeless, untouched by history. This non-involvement in the historical world,[13] the world of societal effects and social movements, directs readings away from dissonantal features which question the timeless verities. Structuralism dichotomizes literature into form and content, and then attends to form and ignores the content, staying within the

14

literature but never effectively dealing with the interface between world and text.[14] The theory introduces a weak and unexamined metaphysic.[15] Much of dissonance occurs at the juncture between history and text, or between form and content, and is lost in an exclusively formalist framework.

Marxism

The interface between the text and the world was scrupulously avoided by formalism, but this juncture was from the outset the central hermeneutical key for Marxist criticism. These critics insisted that the forces which governed history controlled all societal production, including the production of literature. In spite of the many controversies and disagreements between Marxist theorists, there has been fundamental agreement that the events of history when viewed accurately explain literature.

For early theorists, most of literature represented an exact reflection of the oppressive structures in existent societies, illustrating the subjugation of the powerless.[16] Liberating tendencies in literature were also noted. Thus they uncovered and analyzed societal conflicts, and that constituted the act of interpretation.[17] Literature, for these early theorists, serves a didactic function; interpretation demonstrates the truths of Marxist analysis, seeking to uncover and destroy the respectable assumptions of society hidden in literature.

Western Marxism in the 1950's and 1960's cross-pollinated with French Structuralism, and thereby became sensitized to the unique characteristics of literature as an object of examination requiring specialized tools. The Marxist critic was encouraged to distinguish between the oppressive structures in society and the oppressive structures in literature. Literature was allowed its own language, processes, and functions that were not exactly correspondent to similar structures in society. The historical bent of Marxist criticism was not surrendered. Conflicts of society were mediated by literature but not exactly reflected in the text. Literature was a political act but also a uniquely literary one.

Marxist critical thought from these first two periods has offered these insights for an examination of the dissonant text:

1) Marxism introduces a radical historical outlook for the

interpretive task. It insists (contrary to most formalist criticism) that all data, even literary data, must be deeply rooted in the events of history. Literature is therefore a political act. Lukács is largely responsible for the insight that seemingly apolitical positions on literary methodology and epistemology in reality have dramatic political stances implied in their very fabric (Jameson 1972:23-24). To be historically-minded is to attend to the historical causes, however hidden, in the object of study; it is to see the ways in which objects of power (such as literature) have been used by human social institutions to oppress the weak.[18] Unlike Structuralism, Marxism insists that the acts of literature take place within the confines of history, and the interaction between the text and history cannot and must not be ignored.

2) Literature then takes place in history and is subject to constraints comparable to those found in the production of commodities in society.[19] A study of literature must listen to all stages in the production of a literary text, from the supply of its raw materials that shape and are shaped by society (the language and the images or symbols), to the conception (authorial projection or intention), through the actual writing, the reproduction and dissemination, and finally to the reading of the text, as well as to the contexts in which the text is read.

3) The institutions and processes of production in civilization are radically skewed. They produce alienation in the people who make and consume the products. Likewise literature is produced by alienation and produces it as well. Jameson notes: "History is what hurts" (1981:102). "'Writing' is a wrenching; it activates what Derrida characterizes as 'the violence of the letter'" (Raschke 1982:15). The contradictions in the text express this conflict in written form.

4) Literature is *about* these areas of conflict,[20] the inherent contradictions in society. One cannot fully attend to a literary act without hearing the contradictions at its heart.

5) Finally, the oppressive forces of society conceal their activities in layers of "containment"; that is, they protect themselves against the implications of the flaws in their system by producing ideological constructs to conceal the contradictions in a harmonious illusion of wholeness.[21] Literary texts represent

a primary tool used by society to contain the flaws in the cultural construct.

Formalism and Marxism both see the contradiction and concealment of literature. Structuralism stresses the *mediated* nature of literary reality. It does not directly represent the non-textual world, but rather transforms it.[22] Structuralism respects the integrity of literature, allowing it to speak as litera-ture and not as history or analysis of class struggle. Marxism, acknowledging the historical determinations resident in all human acts, insists that the literature, however unique a human artifact, must be compelled to expose its relations to the non-textual fabric of reality.[23]

Deconstruction

Structuralism affirms that texts conceal their central meanings. Deconstruction[24] takes this concept and deepens it into a bitter absence; the text is both schizophrenic and heterogeneous (Jameson 1981:56).[25] It is therefore a collection of disparate elements that cannot and should not be brought together into a harmonious whole. This observation goes beyond the Marxist idea of literature as a tool in an economic and political conflict. Deconstruction asserts that there is no possibility of an absolute horizon, a place where conflict is resolved.[26] There is therefore no chance of escaping the struggle of readings for dominance in society. A "correct" reading is one that is imposed by one group upon another. All readings are largely (if not totally) a reflection of the reader's ideology and efforts to accumulate power. Deconstruction questions the privileged position of any interpretive approach.[27] It follows, therefore, that there is no way to reach the signifier, or even know if there is one to reach (1972:144). All there is is writing (Jameson 1972:184).[28]

Deconstruction holds that any ideological agenda of the literary work is doomed to failure, because inevitably it will be reversed by the other forces active within the text. There is no one point, or one point of view, within a text, and each per-spective contradicts and falsifies the others. There is no center, and the supposed centers are smokescreens for the efforts of parts of the text to exert power over other parts and over the readers.[29]

The interpretive task thus becomes to peel away the layers of deception, of corruption, in an effort to reveal the text as it truly is, a place of contention between conflicting interpretations.[30] One's own interpretation is also suspect in this process of deconstruction.

This reading of texts celebrates an orgy of chaos and heterogeneity (Jameson 1982:56).[31] It abandons the search for an ultimate horizon from which to survey literature. The reader should suspect his or her own motives in interpretation,[32] and thereby distrust any results; one does not attempt interpretation, but celebrates its impossibility.

Deconstruction brings us to the point of seeing all interpretation, all harmonizing impulses, as acts of power that deliberately and systematically conceal the dissonant voices, banishing them from the surface of the text only to find them lurking underneath. Much of writing (and reading as well) consists of attempts to cover up, to conceal the dissonance. However, it refuses to be hidden. It breaks free at the text's weakest points—its seams and its lapses. Winquist (1982:46) notes, "It is in the space of this gap that we sense a surplus of meaning or metaphorical potential for the further determination of meaning." Texts are seldom produced by a single focus of interpretation, but rather emerge from the multiplicity of interpretations which all vie for dominance.

. Reconstructing the text

The text can therefore be reconstructed around the points of dissonance in an act of reading that lends order to the disparate text. "This movement from deconstruction to reconstruction is metaphorical. It does not represent a quest for ultimate meaning, but imaginative play about the text" (Winquist 198:52). Such a paradigm allows the reader to widen his or her critical perspective. Derrida (Spivak 1986:xxviii) notes, "If one is always bound by one's perspective, one can at least deliberately reverse perspectives as often as possible, in the process undoing opposed perspectives, showing that the two terms of an opposition are merely accomplices of each other.'' The text becomes a tool to engage the reader at the point of his or her own ideological confusions.

This reading may be achieved by focusing on:

1) The contribution of formalism, which notes the relationships that the text generates within itself, the structures which reveal the text's hidden meanings.

2) The contribution of Marxism, which analyzes the relationships formed between the text and the various representations of society, the external world, and the attack and defense of social structures which are embodied within the text.

3) The contribution of deconstruction, which highlights the disharmonious contacts, the bumpings, scrapings, clashings and grindings. Where things do not fit, or where they are forcibly driven underground—this is the object of investigation.

4) The disruption, the dissonance, is the stuff with which literature functions. The act of focusing literature around the dissonant structural features is the reconstruction of the text. This pronouncement is by no means meant to imply that deconstruction ends with this act of reconstruction. The text continues to clash with all imposed readings, including this one, constantly generating fresh manifestations of literature's liberating impulse. As Spivak notes (1986:lxx-lxxi), ''It is not easy to coin a word without seeming to privilege it as a term of final reference.''

Herein lies a method appropriate for examining a text that is characteristically disparate. In the sections that follow, I will expose the approach in more detail, and demonstrate its appropriateness to an analysis of the book of Job.

LOCATING AND IDENTIFYING DISSONANCE

The text is the site of conflict. It is the juncture of forces that impinge upon the act of reading, and each of these forces is a source of disharmonic elements that resist sense, resist aggressive interpretation. Spivak (1986:lxxv) notes, ''If in the process of deciphering a text in the traditional way we come across a word that seems to harbor an unresolvable contradiction, and by virtue of being one word is made sometimes to work in one way and sometimes in another and thus is made to point away from the absence of a unified meaning, we shall catch at the word." These points of juncture are examples of potential dissonance created in the production of literature.[33]

Society and Author

The society, the culture as a whole, and the power structures that stand behind and support the institutions are inevitably[34] at odds with the author or authors,[35] those most directly responsible for the planning and fabrication of texts. Various social institutions provide symbols, the raw material of the author's reflections. The author works with symbols to create a literary text. But symbols resist reduction into particular manifestations of language. They are by nature general, their influence felt powerfully in the thinking of society but not wholly present in any one place.

When an author encodes symbols by using them to describe a certain narrative or poetic situation, he or she does violence to the integrity of the symbol. No longer is it a pervasive yet unexamined influence, but rather is contained in the confines of written language.[36] The symbol is necessarily changed. Language-encoding reduces the symbol. It has less influence and power than it had previously possessed. Now it can be examined, its implications questioned. Even in cases where the author sets out to support the ideological constraints of society, the act of writing highlights the flaws in societal assumptions, and leads to the deconstruction of those assumptions.

The reification of symbols is not the only source of conflict. The author him- or herself contributes to the text's conflict with society. He or she writes out of a sense of pain, of dislocation, a feeling of wrongness in his or her universe, either to call attention to the wrongness, or to conceal it. Clearly, a person in harmony seldom writes, and what he or she writes is seldom read by others. It is when the pain in the writer resonates with the pain of readers or consumers of literature that a work is widely disseminated. This is not to say that all literature is revolutionary. Rather, most literature is expressly intended to conceal the disruption, to make it all better. The fact of pain, though, is always there, and this pain is in conflict with the societal illusion of harmony and certainty.[37] Whether as a cry of pain or an elaborate cover-up, dislocation is the primary motivation for literature's production.

The distribution and consumption of literature, seldom examined in criticism, contributes significantly to what the author writes. What the author writes, and what he or she wants to write might be—and often are—two different things because most writers want above all to be read.[38] In order to be read, the writer must align him- or herself with a distribution network, in ancient as well as modern contexts. Because these networks are usually controlled by ruling groups in the culture,[39] the author conforms (often subconsciously) to societal expectations in order to retain any possibility of influence. The work can seldom be overtly radical. Therefore, the author will often express resistance to the reality-picture that is imposed upon the literary task, hoping to retain integrity. Although supporting societal assumptions on a superficial level in order to be read, he or she questions them covertly.

Author and Individual Reader

The author's reading conflicts with other readings that the text generates. The author has a particular projection of what that text must say, but because of the separation between the author and his or her work, readers resist this projection. The text is cut loose from the author and interacts with readers independent of its parent. This is particularly true in ancient texts such as the Hebrew Bible, due to their long and varied history of transmission. The text comes to say things the author did not want to say, sometimes says things the author intended to conceal, and sometimes says things of which the author was not remotely aware. In any case, authorial intention (which has been seen as the key to the understanding of text) is often at odds with what the text actually accomplishes. "Authorial intention is not invalid as a point in the production of literature, but is rather largely ineffective. Much is included that the writer did not intend, and much gets in against the writer's intention," (Macherey 1978:258).

The reader receives messages from a text that relate not only to the actual signs read but also to the expectations and views of the reader as a literary consumer. This consumer imposes his or her world upon the text, ignoring or misconstruing authorial projection. In the ancient world, where the process by which a text gains fixity is long and drawn-out, readers actually change a text to conform with later societal expectations and needs. The reader reforms the author into his or her image. Conflict exists at the juncture between the author's reading (writing) of the text and later readings.

In the situation of a long-enduring text, successive readings seek to displace earlier ones, producing a conflict between readings. Later readings reconstrue texts, relating them to current concerns. Readers allegorize, doing violence to early usages of the material, and remove it further from the author's world.

Society and Text

Society reproduces texts, choosing which ones it will disseminate, for reasons that are seldom explicit. Cultural representatives edit and change the text into something more "contemporary." "A text is not a finished product, but is an ongoing production which continuously emerges in and through the activity of interpretation," (Taylor 1969:66-67). In the ancient world particularly, scribal interference affects considerably the development of texts. This is achieved through efforts to anthologize, and juxtapose the text with others, thus transforming genre so as to change the meaning of the parts in relation to a newly constituted whole. When scribes placed a text into a new context, this dramatically reordered the meaning which thus became contingent upon the neighboring material. "The work never 'arrives unaccompanied'; it is always determined by the existence of other works, which can belong to different areas of production. There is no first book, independent and absolutely innocent. . . Thus the book is always the site of an exchange" (Macherey 1978:100). Certain social groups control the tools of publishing, whether linotype press or papyrus, and exclude outsiders. Ancient priests even kept the knowledge of writing as their exclusive domain. In cultures that allow a mass-distribution, the social distinctions of language itself become exclusionary tools, with a "higher" and "lower" literature, the "higher" encoded and unavailable to the great mass of society. The formation and usage of language itself becomes a source of conflict and social manipulation.

Societal and Individual Readings

There is a conflict between the communal reading and the individual reading, between ideology (which represents the stated needs of the community) and personal experience. Interest groups that support the institutions of that society seek to impose particular ideological readings upon the individual. The individual reader encounters places where the literary world (the world contained within the text) differs from the world of personal experience. Such textual dislocation is disturbing.

The book of Job recounts a struggle between the prevailing theological construct that God punishes sin and rewards righteousness, and the individual and corporate experience of undeserved disaster. Likewise, a black slave in North America, hearing the account of the slaves in Exodus, would experience conflict between sanctioned slavery and the liberation of Israelite slaves. When non-textual reality contradicts the ideological framework of the text, dissonance results.

Dissonance and the Act of Reading

Dissonance is found at the junctures within the confines of the text itself, in the seams that divide the text into parts, or join text to text. The polymorphous text of Job has many such junctures. They produce failures of sense and create resistance to genetic classification.[40]

There are also logical seams, fault-lines between the text and the idea of "sense" in the mind of the reader. This might not correspond to particular historical developments in the text. The conflicts and unanswered questions that arise as a result of reading provide important material for examination. As men-

tioned above, successive readings of older texts seek to allegorize and to make them relevant for the contemporary community.[41] In places where the text resists this allegorization, where
it seems to want to go in another direction, dissonance occurs.

Dissonance arises at the point where ideology's harmonizing
impulse fails to make sense of the text. What a text does not say
and what readers avoid reading become the objects of examination. Many points within texts disturb readers, who then develop
elaborate interpretive devices to avoid noting these points.
When important textual features are never mentioned or are
carefully explained and thus contained, one usually finds
dissonance.

DISSONANCE AS AN INTERPRETIVE KEY

Dissonance points to concealment. Concealment occurs during
all aspects of literary production; those who write, disseminate,
read and analyze the text all engage in acts of concealment.
While vested interests seek to guide the interpretation of texts
along conventional lines, disparate features enable the critic to
unmask hermeneutical dishonesty, the dynamics of oppression
in a literary work.

Conflicting elements enable the critic to understand the
relationships among the literary sections and to decode the
processes of literary production and textual function. All too
often a critic or reader will isolate a particular textual feature
(history, author, internal textual dynamics, among others) and
ignore the complex relations among features. But this interaction among the elements produces the text. Individual features
exist only in relationship to the whole and the other parts. An
examination of dissonance will reveal the relationships, whether
of harmony or incongruity, sense or nonsense.[42]

The text speaks powerfully and authentically from the place
of dissonance.[43] It asserts two or more contrary things together, the synthesis passing on to a new level of discourse. There
forms an horizon from which to view literature. This enables
one to overcome to a significant degree the ideological constraints which prevent reading from being fresh and emancipa-
tory. Finally, by deconstructing some of the central conflicts in

the writing, one sees literature as an actual and important participant in the processes of history; not as a mere reflection but a powerful force for oppression. Occasionally, in subtle ways, a text may be a force for liberation (usually through irony or surreptitious juxtaposition of disparate parts).

Through examination of dissonance, a text confronts the contemporary reader and the contemporary culture. This approach enables it to speak to cultures and civilizations alien to its original context. Almost inevitably, to "modernize" a text is to distort it, to compel its continuity with the modern world. This is mitigated by examining both the continuity and particularly the discontinuity between the contemporary world of the twentieth century interpreter and (in our case) the ancient Near Eastern world. The text can thereby speak and we can listen in more honest and less manipulative ways.

DISSONANCE IN JOB

Job, with its confluence of genres, highlights the phenomenon of dissonance particularly well. Job's dissonance reflects a number of societal struggles which can be elucidated by an examination of the textual conflict. The sapiential movement in Israel was often at odds with the other segments of Israelite society. A similar conflict between the sages and other segments of society occurred in both Ancient Egypt and Babylon. The intelligentsia in every age have an awkward and complex relationship with the ruling powers. The ideological disparity of Job reflects this tension, also opening up debates within the community of the sages itself.

Later interpretations of Job have attempted to impose harmony on the text, and have greatly transformed subsequent understandings of the book. Many readings of Job have been particularly weak throughout the history of its analysis. Both ancient and modern "pre-critical" approaches to Job have sought by the suppression of one of the parts to generate a coherent and unified statement out of Job.

This effort has been joined by the new "literary critics" of the Hebrew Bible who through a sophisticated view of repeating motifs seek to prove that Job is a seamless garment. The critical approach to Job has similarly ignored key features of the book, in this case, the effect that the book as a whole has had upon its various audiences. The valid and relevant search to understand the historical background of the disparate parts of this book have not been adequately supplemented by a desire to examine the effects of juxtaposition. This too must be done if one would gain a deeper understanding of the book of Job.

Was dissonance in Job primarily an inadvertent effect or did the authors (those who participated in the process of the work's production) deliberately sabotage the sense of the work in order to attack the generally accepted ideology of Israel?[44] In the case of Job, this dissonance was deliberate, but not on the part of a single individual. Rather, the social realities generated by the conflicting interpretive communities produced the dissonantal features. The overall effect is not the act of a single individual or group.

The moral concerns in Job are of particular interest in the modern world, existing as it does after the Holocaust and in the shadow of the nuclear threat. This analysis goes beyond the formal problem of dissonance in Job. One reads the text of reality and *it* is dissonant. Should not dissonantal texts reflect this? The text therefore becomes the means by which we may explore ourselves and our world.

An irrational universe impinges upon our attempt to order our lives. Therein lies our innate need to cope with conflict and find a means to understand dissonance. Although it is imperative to avoid distorting a text to reflect our own interests, one might select texts that seem to address problems that are relevant to contemporary concerns. Job is such a text.

2

COMPOSITION
AND
DISSONANCE

ESTABLISHING THE DISSONANCE

The chief dissonantal feature of Job is the shocking disparity between the frame (chapters 1, 2 and 42:7-17) and the center.[1] Virtually everyone acknowledges that sharp divergences in style exist between the parts. A compelling, although less widely accepted, consensus exists that these stylistic differences manifest significant theological distinctions.

The center uses poetry as its primary mode of communication. The frame employs prose. They have different vocabularies, and use different terms for the deity. "We would only point out that the obvious and drastic difference between the idyllic, stylized character of the narrative and the passionate, existential creativity of the poetry, places a virtually unbearable burden of proof upon anyone who would resist seeing evidence of two literary hands—indeed, of two literary worlds" (Moore 1983:18). Terrien observes (1954:877, 875). "While the poem presents the most peculiar language of the Old Testament, being filled with words of Aramaic, Arabic, Akkadian, and even Egyptian origin, the narrative is written in pure, classical Hebrew." Hurvitz (197:18) has argued convincingly for the presence of late Hebrew vocabulary in the frame, but this can as easily be accounted for through the editing efforts of the later tradents as by a completely late origination.

The center communicates through long, reflective dialogues, but narrative action and formal speech characterize the frame. Ancient literatures tend toward repetition more than do modern genres. The center repeats ideas by saying the same thing in many different ways but, by contrast, the frame repeats action.

Dramatically different theological sensibilities characterize the two parts. The center contains much more rebellion and skepticism than does the frame. One text presents a pious[2], patient and orthodox Job, the other a Job railing against God.[3] The texts likewise reveal two radically distinct gods. An insecure and petulant god is portrayed in the frame, particularly the prologue; a thundering and majestic (blustering) god appears in the center and is reflected in the other sections (Vogels 1980: 835-836).

The center is abstract and evidences little action. It is longer and more verbose than the frame. Most popular readings recount the story of Job as if the middle chapters did not exist. The story of the frame endures in the minds of most readers, and provides the primary interpretive key to the whole. In contrast, most scholars largely ignore the frame. An interesting recent example of this is René Girard's, *Job, the Victim of His People* (1987:76). He refers to the frame as "the false prologue and conclusion" (46). "The friends are not there to comfort Job as the prologue has the *gall* to proclaim" [emphasis added]. "The prologue and the conclusion [along with the speeches of Yahweh] eliminate the essential and make the Dialogues unreadable, to transform the book of Job into a ludicrous anecdote recited mechanically by everyone" (142).

Scarcely any monographs have been written on the frame;[4] most emphasis is on the center. Commentaries usually relegate these three chapters to a minor role in the movement of the book. For example, Dhorme proclaims (1967:lxiv): "The monument which the author aims at creating is the poem. The Prologue and Epilogue are no more than its entrance and exit." The new "literary critical" commentaries: Marvin H. Pope (1973); Norman C. Habel (1985); J. Gerald Janzen (1985), while conceding the literary importance of the frame, see its value only in its demonstrated consistency with the center which is acknowledged as the true source of inspiration for the book. In contrast, the various religious communities have largely emphasized the narrative of the frame.

One cannot therefore embrace the book in its entirety as representing a single angle of vision. Whether because of the theological naivety or inferiority[5] of the frame or for any of a number of other reasons, the parts oppose each other at many points. Both the scholarly and confessional community find it difficult to take the frame and center together as a single unified work.

How can we account for this disparity?[6] A stylistic explanation implies that the same author wrote both at roughly the same time, varying the parts for a more overriding dramatic purpose. A historical explanation accounts for the differences by pointing to distinct contexts for each part, each originating from different communities or individuals.

If one posits a unitary authorship, the conflicts between the parts must be explained as skillful variations in style. Those who seek to demonstrate these differences as artistic variation (certainly possible in other circumstances) point to the similarity of concerns[7] and to the linguistic and thematic reflections of the center found in the frame (Dhorme 1967:lxi-lxii).[8] Such observations highlight the assumptions of the commentators more than they elucidate the text itself.[9] They attempt to account for the differences without surrendering the ideological assumptions of the unified text. There are theological, philosophical and political reasons why critics desire such a unified text; one finds ulterior motives that do not result from an "objective" examination of the text. Rather, these theories are suggested by special ideological interests. Theologically, a unified text which says only one thing, however complex, supports the view of a single comprehensible God speaking through the scriptures. Philosophically, a unified text affirms that truth communicates most effectively through logical, non-contradictory propositional statements. Politically, a text that speaks with one voice will most commonly reflect the will of the controlling tradents and suppress whatever dissenting voices might have influenced the textual transmission. The differences, however, so profound and pervasive, are more easily explained as a radical reworking of previously existing material.

Some have speculated that the same individual wrote the two parts: the frame, composed earlier in the author's artistic career, and the dialogues in a later, more mature period of life. This argument concedes that the two parts are indeed different and reflect distinct historical periods. But there is nothing in the dialogue found also in the frame that could not be explained more plausibly by simple literary dependence, rather than shared authorship.

The historical explanation for dissonance presents a stronger case. It offers two options. Some have argued that the center was written first and the frame was penned later to give a narrative context to the poetic dialogue. It makes more sense however, to view the dialogue as a further development flowing out of the ancient story than to imagine a truncated dialogue craving and then generating an accompanying story that would give it narrative weight. I follow Janzen, who reasons that,

> It is impossible. . . to strip away the prologue and the epilogue and to read the dialogues by themselves. The poetry cannot be supposed to have existed in such a form, for it requires the prologue to set the scene for its own intense dialogical questioning. Either the prose sections were composed for specific literary effects by the author of the poetry or, *what amounts to the same thing*, [emphasis added] the poet adopted (or adapted) for fresh purposes a story already extant in some form (Janzen 1985:23).[10]

DATING THE DISSONANCE

By process of elimination, the most likely historical reconstruction of Job asserts that some form of the frame existed before the center was written. More specific attempts to date the two parts betray fundamental weaknesses in methodology and reasoning.[11] One must therefore establish an adequate method of dating the respective parts in order to account for the conflict between them.[12]

No direct historical references exist in either the frame or the center that would enable us to place them at specific points in the history of Israel (Roberts 1977:109).[13] Some have therefore concluded that attempts to date the sections of Job are exercises in futility. Job, they say, is a universal work that cannot be limited by means of dating to a particular time or place. Rather it is synchronic, relevant for all peoples in the same way.[14] The critic's refusal to date the book, however, tears it from its historical context and diminishes the value of subsequent interpretive work. Literary texts necessarily interact with all levels of society.[15]

Inherent weaknesses occur in all of the traditional attempts to date the book of Job. They base the broadest conclusions on relatively flimsy and speculative evidence. The frame probably has chronological priority, but the means for demonstrating this conclusion are inadequate.

Are there any more substantial clues as to the transmissional history of the text? Two irreducible features of the Joban text as it now exists (henceforth referred to as "the canonical Job") provide important indications of its historical development. The first is a feature of the text, the second a feature of the analysis of the text. The first is commentary, a discussion of the disparity between the parts; the second, metacommentary, a disparity between the various interpretations.

The first irreducible feature, an aspect of the text, is the continued presence of the pious Job, who is at odds with the rebellious Job of the center. Pious Job clearly represents the ideologically dominant aspect of the book. The second is that an examination of Joban interpreters, indicates their inability to determine Job's historical context.[16] These two components highlight deep-seated conflicts at the very heart of the text. These conflicts, in turn, enable us to uncover the societal tensions produced by the book's collision with various Israelite institutions.

The first irreducible Joban element is the enduring image of the patient and pious Job. The two pictures of Job cannot be reconciled because they come from significantly different cultures, each maintaining viability within the complex text regardless of any attempts on the part of tradents or interpreters to quiet one or the other. The presence of this hapless figure suggests the existence of a legendary Job behind the frame narrative. This figure of oral storytelling continues to influence interpretation of the canonical text, persisting in contemporary interpretation. Ancient oral tales commonly retain this power over later treatments of their material. This is due to their cultural and emotive resonance with some of the most formative notions of society, and to the narrative skill that was employed in their construction, resulting from generations of refinement.

The conflict between the pious Job of the frame and the blasphemous Job in the center reveals the central tension with which the late tradent had to deal. On the one hand, the theological tensions implicit in the original story inspired the tradent to work with it, to transform it into something different, a more profound protest against the theological power structure of the day. On the other hand, the facile piety on the surface conflicted with the fundamental theological presuppositions of the tradent. The tradent could not respond without creating a different Job, a different God, both derivative and contradictory.

A legendary Job necessarily existed because of the continued existence of this picture in the text and in popular interpretation of the text, in spite of the fact that the great majority of the material develops in a dramatically different fashion.

This legendary Job functions in two ways in the societies that tell the story. First, it confirms the easy piety of the superficially religious, reaffirming the control of the religious establishment. It supports the status quo of religion and justifies the triumphalist God. Second, it generates the tension that produced the canonical Job, because it says more than it seems. Legendary Job has a historical origin, but also a continued existence embedded in the text.

The striking absence of clear historical references leads reputable critics using similar approaches to develop radically divergent conclusions as to the dating of the various parts of Job. In all three areas of inquiry, markedly different conclusions are drawn concerning Job's historical context based on linguistic, stylistic and theological grounds.

The setting of Job takes place outside of Israel, thus adding to the historical ambiguity, achieving a deliberate distancing of the material from a contemporary cultic or political context. The presence of obsessive historical preoccupation in the exilic and post-exilic period would likely generate its counterpart, either offering a dissenting theological explanation of history such as the apocalyptic world view, or else avoiding historical motifs altogether. The authors of the book of Job have picked this second option. Such concealment is deliberate.

Duquoc comes closest to examining this chronological concealment as an ideological effort by the author of Job's center. He notes this avoidance of history as an attempt to assert that:

> The God of Israel may not be wholly contained within the prophets' moral message. . . The author of the Book of Job, by placing his theological debate outside the period of the rewriting and outside the sacred space of biblical territory, was able to make himself the echo of the idea taking shape in the ambiguous stories which the priestly tidiers were trying to purge (Duquoc 1983:83).[17]

The late redactor of Job resists reliable dating as a protest against the interpretive order imposed by both the prophetic and priestly classes in Israel. By avoiding the popular historical interpretive systems of Israel, covenantal theology and deutero-nomistic explanations, this writer looked back upon the legendary period of Israel, when things were not so centrally controlled. The author protested against those who believed that Israel's dilemma was explainable in the theological terms that supported the ideologies of Israel's dominant groups. History had been appropriated by the theologians of the post-exilic period. This was embodied by the prophets' optimistic revisions of the tragic events in Israel's history, and especially by the priestly "tidiers" who were diligently re-editing the old stories of ancient Israel, infusing them with the new ideology of the post-exilic period, characterized by exclusivism, rigid cultic observances, and a complete centralization of political, economic and religious life.

Canonical Job protested against such theologies of explanation which claimed that, starting with a theological premise, one might explain everything in terms of that premise regardless of experience. Israel's experience was one of suffering, and these theologies failed to demonstrate an adequate grasp of that reality, either minimizing or denying it. By recourse to history, these theologians claimed that every terrible thing that happened to Israel had an explanation, and that this explanation relieved God of responsibility. They preserved God's reputation by removing him from the human sphere, replacing him with a strict law of retribution. The final form of the book of Job embodies a reaction against the historical interpretations of the author's contemporaries. This absence of historical reference is a key datable feature of the book.[18]

Historical critics seek clues that will indicate a particular period in Israel's history. Job resists this, which is not to say that Job is not historically rooted, but rather that these roots are concealed so skillfully that attempts to date from the perspective of historical criticism inevitably fail. The key historical-critical feature that leads to an adequate dating of the material is the text's resistance of dating.

The legendary Job will not be harmonized with the Job of the center, just as the canonical Job will not be dated using the traditional methods. The book of Job resists two of the primary literary impulses that have served biblical commentators in analyzing biblical texts—the urge to explain historically and the impulse to harmonize. Critics work so hard to resolve the difficulties that they do not pause to explore the unique shapes of those difficulties which may provide access points to the ideologies at conflict within the text.

Lacking unambiguous chronological markers, we must develop a heuristic model to describe the development of Job from its literary progenitor to the canonical Job. It becomes necessary to construct imaginatively a model that would account for the present condition of the text.

THE TRANSMISSIONAL HISTORY OF JOB

The legendary Job

Before the book of Job was finalized in canonical form, there was a legendary Job.[19] A story, whether oral or written, had some prominence within the Hebrew society of the monarchy.[20] It was likely a point of study and discussion among the sages of many cultures.[21] The Hebrews translated the story fully into their own cultural concepts, and in so doing they allowed the characters depicted to gain a tremendous complexity, especially in the depiction of the deity. This story never offered unqualified support for the societal assumptions of Israel's theologians, but always retained a note of questioning, of irony, even of mocking. Its seeming adherence to the accepted covenantal ideas only concealed its deeper questioning. Ernst Bloch (1972:14) calls it "subversive slave talk." The seeds of dissent were contained within its structural elements.

This narrative roughly corresponds to the frame in the canonical book of Job.[22] The sages told this story to the people and discussed it among themselves. It served as a basis for their considerations of the nature of reality, as a palette they could use to paint their intellectual creations. Legendary Job reflected their intellectual concerns and became one of the texts that expressed and shaped the sapiential agenda.

One would like to examine how this folk story functioned in Israelite society, but many barriers obstruct a reliable determination. The story today exists as part of a larger whole, dislocated from that original context. There is no reliable way to ascertain what parts of the Masoretic text of Job actually were a part of the original folk story.[23]

Most re-creations of the folk story approach the text by assuming that those aspects which seem most archaic, the repetitive, the mythic, or those thought to reflect a more "primitive" view of God represent the original folk story.[24] Others try to reduce the story to a minimal skeleton of narrative structure, those elements without which we would have no story, and call this the folk story.[25]

From the internal evidence, the folk story can be tentatively reconstructed as follows: A man thought righteous and deserving of blessing loses all that he possesses, and ultimately, his health as well. He remains faithful and obedient throughout. He is ultimately restored to a place of greater blessing than he possessed formerly, vindicated by the deity who had afflicted him.

The folk story *did not* contain the long poetic dialogues that are found in chapters 3-42:6, although it probably mentioned the individuals, Eliphaz, Bildad, and Zophar.[26] We don't know what the friends did in the original story because all they do in the present editions is what occurs in chapter 2 and the epilogue—they sit with him in silence, and Yahweh rebukes them. One must therefore assume that something is missing from the folk story, a movement of narrative that is implied in the original, but which has been replaced by the poetic dialogues. The later editor removed the original activities of the friends and inserted the center.

The presence of the Satan, Job's wife,[27] and the angels is in dispute. In fact, the wife's role expands in the Septuagint and "the Testament of Job," indicating its lack of fixity as the work develops (Spittler 1983, chaps. 21-25). The angels are thought to come either from ancient primitive mythology of the divine court, or from a Persian pantheon, proving either their antiquity or modern innovations. Historical ambiguity abounds in the features of the book.

The folk story, thus reconstructed, embodies at first glance a simple piety. God inflicts a terrible testing upon a faithful individual. Piety is rewarded; the universe remains a predictable and secure place. However, even at this point, the story contains significant components of irony.[28] Its ancient picture cannot be perfectly merged with the later Israelite ideas of retributive theology or centrist piety. The text of legendary Job contains many seditious elements which provide the occasion for its use by the later tradent of Job.[29] This ancient tale examined the fundamental assumptions behind the mechanisms of piety and retributive justice. The very act of such reflection implies a reversal of authority; those principles used to sift and judge Israel are now in turn examined. The radical nature of the center is therefore implicit in the story's earliest form.

Implied in the folk story are the following ideas that question Israel's most fundamental notions:

1) The text pictures God in a negative, weak manner.[30] The Satan tricked him into destroying his servant, and then God came to blame the Satan for enticing him[31] to destroy Job "without cause." Paul Weiss (1969:182-183) states, "A childishly conceived God, a childlike God . . . proceeds to do almost everything the most villainous of beings could want." Gilbert Murray (1969:195) observes, "It is like torturing your faithful dog to see if you can make him bite you." Then God thought naively that everything could be made better by giving Job back what he lost. Meir Weiss (1983:37) quotes the Talmud: "Were it not written in the Bible it would be impossible to say: God is like a man whom someone tries to incite and who is in the end incited." Habel (80), describes Yahweh in the frame "as a less than average human being with a great deal of power, a small-minded king that everybody has to humor."

2) The Satan was more clever than God, able to manipulate the deity for his own purposes. Yahweh thereby loses majesty. Bloch (1972:119) says, "To all these white-washing theodicies Job would have replied: Yahweh cannot be both almighty and good if he gives Satan free rein. He can only be almighty and evil, or good and weak." Kluger (1967:81) notes that psychologically, as opposed to theologically, "[The Satan] is really stronger."

3) Job's servile obedience in the face of such blatant mistreatment is less than admirable. Stephen Mitchell (1987:348) observes "The character called 'The Lord' can do anything to him—have his daughters raped and mutilated, send his sons to Auschwitz—and he will turn the other cheek. This is not a matter of spiritual acquiescence, but of mere capitulation to an unjust, superior force." Is it possible to imagine that ancient people would not also resent such unrealistic piety?

4) The unacceptably abrupt restoration of Job does not adequately recompense Job for all his suffering.[32] The addition of the more skeptical dialogues to the book of Job is ample evidence that some significant portion of ancient Israel's intellectual community did not accept the easy answers that seem to proceed from the earliest edition of Job.

5) Contrary to what is commonly believed, the frame does not unequivocally support the law of retribution. Job's willingness to receive "evil from Yahweh" as well as the good, questions some of the chief views of Israelite theology on the predictability of God.[33]

From these irregularities we see the existence of irony within the folk story which lies behind the frame. This irony accentuates the importance of this portion of Job.[34] Both for its impact on Israelite society in its original narrative form, as well as upon the later transmissional history of the book, the frame's vital contributions have been largely ignored by the scholarly community.

However, the poet considered the frame of particular worth and importance, so that it was preserved largely intact. Or perhaps societal constraints compelled the author to retain it. At any rate, the narrative frame generates considerable interest on its own, and the popular uses of the book have usually centered on the story with its simple lessons in piety, rather than the anguished cry of the material of the center. The more subtle ironies in the frame have often been overlooked, but the *story* of the frame has consistently struck a responsive chord in generations of readers and hearers.[35]

The juxtaposition of the center and the frame in a single work requires us to hear them together if for no other reason than because they speak in proximity. Many ideas and themes are addressed by both.[36] Each piece should not be viewed in isolation, as if the reader were ignorant of the other. A study of the book of Job must acknowledge the frame, not ignore it or relegate it to the realm of the unimportant.

General critical theory would assert the frame's importance. It gives form and shape to the story, and carries hidden meanings, things concealed either consciously or unconsciously by the writers and tradents. It serves as a medium of communication, bearing the same (or contrary) message as the poetic center, but in more subtle and significantly revealing ways.

The frame is often found to be at odds with the poetic center. As such it provides considerable perspective on what the author of the dialogues did not state overtly. Therefore, this

earlier material is as significant as the efforts of the later tradent, and in refined and subtle ways it expresses rebellion
against commonly accepted notions of God in relation to humanity. The legendary material has persisted in the hearts of the
people, whereas the center has primarily been a subject for
scholarly debate. The frame is far more subversive for being on
the surface such a pious conceit. Its ancient legendary form,
refined by centuries of oral transmission through the cultural
filters of many societies, expresses a power unmatched by the
eloquence and erudition of the center.

The later tradent is indeed yet another attempt to silence
the powerful voice of the legendary Job. The tradent engages in
a well-meaning act of censorship, attempting to explicate the
radical criticism already implicit in the legendary Job. As with
most attempts to clarify a narrative intellectually, the attempt
fails, only layering the text in greater obfuscation and conflict.
The legendary Job stands out as a powerful and effective voice,
the efforts to silence the tale only highlighting its power.[37]

Added Dialogue and Transformed Frame

At some point this story, whether in written or oral form, became a forum for controversy in the Israelite sapiential community (Good 1973:472). Consequently a particular sage wrote an
extended series of poetic dialogues, either replacing or imagin-
ing what Job's friends must have said to him, and what he
would have said in return.[38] It is impossible to determine when
this took place. The sage wrote the poems to complete and
elaborate the theological insights in the folk story, using the
previous story-line, and infusing it with a new theological and
historical point of view by putting the issues of suffering and
piety into a sharper perspective. The writer gives the dialogue
of the friends a conventional form. Job alternates with his
friends in three cycles of dialogues. The third dialogue appears
truncated in present editions. Some critics insist that such
textual disruption is due to stylistic design, namely the encroaching of chaos upon the arguments of the friends. More
likely, however, an editor either intentionally or unintentionally

changed the text. If intentionally, it might imply that Job's speeches were found unacceptable by this later scribe.

Not part of this rigid structure, but probably part of the same construction, are the speeches of Yahweh, encompassing chapters 38 through 42:6.[39] The Elihu speeches function in the present text as unintentional comic relief and were certainly added later by some pious soul desperate to rescue and improve upon the arguments of the friends (Robertson 1977: 47-48).[40]

Finally, there is chapter 28, a hymn to the inaccessibility of wisdom. Its message conforms with the struggles of Job, but its style and voice hold no place in the narrative movement. Probably this poem was inserted because of its pertinence to certain issues at question. Because this hymn and Elihu's superficial piety reflect religious attitudes at any period, it is difficult to date them or compare their relative influence on the text. In any case, that influence was slight.

Although the narrative power of legendary Job continues unabated, the writer of the center would certainly contend that the dialogues constitute the literary center of the book of Job. Furthermore, the present received text bears ample evidence of that fact, both in its length, heights of eloquence, and the complexity and seriousness of its argument.[41]

From the moment that the two main sections were wedded, it seems, scholarly attention was drawn to the literary weight of the center. Legendary Job and the Job of the poetic center are somehow allies. They each fight against a similar enemy, although in different ways. They struggle against each other but mostly against their own surroundings. Macherey notes, "the use of [an] ancient story brings to the forefront the conflict between a society and its ancient literature" (Macherey 1978: 234). This conflict describes the struggle of each new cultural context to incorporate the insights of the old one.

THE HISTORICAL NATURE OF DISSONANCE IN JOB

Conflict therefore defines Job. Society attempts to tame legendary Job by reading it as a simple pious statement of a person's faithfulness in the face of repeated temptations to forsake God, and how he is rewarded in the end. The frame resists such a reading, and one cannot remove the objectionable elements without destroying the fabric of the text.

The tradent attempts to tame legendary Job by making explicit what was implicit, by saying philosophically and theologically what had been said differently and perhaps more effectively in a narrative fashion. Stories tend to involve readers more than discourse. This is true even where the discourse is as exalted and poetic as the center of Job. This appropriation agrees with the theological perspective of the legendary Job, but attempts to translate its message into a different cultural and philosophical context.[42]

This is not to say that all attempts to rework an ancient "pristine" text (whether oral or written) are by definition invalid and inappropriate. Rather, these particular attempts fail to conceal the original narrative strength of legendary Job.

A new and exciting work results, one that now highlights these conflicts, these new attempts to use the text, and the text's resistance to them. Canonical Job is now about these conflicts, which dramatically elucidate the concerns of legendary Job, the conflict between interpretation and reality.

3

DISSONANCE
AND
POINTS
OF
ACCESS

The clash between the various elements of literature including not only the text but its production and consumption as well, provides a key to understanding not what literature means but how it functions, what it does as it passes through society. Such a dissonant passage is a rough journey, and the scars of the journey impress themselves upon the text.[1]

The book of Job, divided historically between frame and center, nevertheless impinges upon the reader as a complex whole. This binary division between the revolutionary text and the appropriated text can be more fully explained. The reader's juxtaposing of texts within the text creates many new configurations that, although not determined by a particular author or editor,[2] may reflect the ideological dimensions of the text and its readings more fully than a purely historical (transmissional) exploration would do. The larger text's lack of smoothness points to conflicting forces under the surface that do not permit a completely harmonizing interpretation. Winquist (1982:54) says, "The collision or overlay of dissimilar texts will often cancel out parts and isolate images that claim our attention and draw us into their extralinguistic isolation."

NEW CONFIGURATIONS IN CANONICAL JOB

The placement of the poetic center in the midst of the legendary Job tale, the frame, creates an entirely new work that consists of four parts rather than two. These parts interact in a series of shifting, unstable alliances.[3] The frame, split in two, becomes the prologue and epilogue of the newly created work. The center (excluding for the moment the speeches of Elihu and the hymn to wisdom) also contains two parts, the dialogue between Job and his friends, and the speeches of Yahweh. These four parts relate to each other in shifting patterns of signification, and the cracks created in the narrative produce new readings which interact with various hermeneutic communities.

While in legendary Job, the frame, a simple piety is both praised and undermined, one should not conclude that the prologue and the epilogue of the book of Job necessarily support the simple pious positions that were found in the original story.[4] Likewise, although the center as a whole reflects a highly ironic and skeptical view of late Israelite theology, one must not thereby assume that the two parts of the center necessarily take a skeptical position in contradistinction to the frame. The strict dichotomy between the frame and the center, discussed in chapter 2, is broken. A new tension is created.

As a result of these shifting patterns, there are profound breakdowns in the narrative movement, both between these four created parts and within individual parts, when the reader takes into account their juxtaposition within the narrative whole.

Although Job is not a unified whole, as many have claimed, it stands now as a single narrative unit: first by intention, because the final editor put the disparate parts together to intend a single textual event; and second, by virtue of the reading, because people read a single book that is collected under the title *Job*. Certainly most of the parts concern the profound sufferings of a man named Job in the distant past, and this central character leads readers to impose some kind of narrative unity on the story of the text.[5]

A reader reads a text by seeking a harmony which reflects his or her unique ideological slant. Job thwarts this expectation of unified narration at many key points. These points provide places of access that uncover the hidden ideological activity within the text and in readings of the text.[6] These various faults, absences of expected resolution, provide keys to understanding the text of Job. They will be examined in turn.

PIOUS AND BLASPHEMOUS JOB

Who is Job? Our sympathies rest with him throughout his many turns in the narrative, but his persona keeps changing,[7] not as a developing character but rather as an elusive figure. In chapter 2 the strong clash between the Job of the prologue and the Job of the center was explored. Whereas piety describes the figure in the folk tale, the Job of the poetry blasphemes. The juxtaposition of these two sections, these two Jobs, creates a new reality, one that says both more and less than the parts.[8]

These two positions are not opposites, nor are they mutually exclusive. The poet rather took issues raised by the frame, and carried them further. He or she did not correct the frame but clarified it. The two sections imply other possibilities, perhaps not considered or deliberately suppressed by their creators. In the case of the frame, both the retributive orthodoxy as well as a less fastidious reaction to disaster are implied by the text. These counterpoints to the folk tale, present as ghosts that inform the reading or telling of this narrative, dramatically influenced the production of the center. The center itself continually echoes a naive faith underneath its words, a hope that things might not be as bad as Job imagines. Also, a rejection of meaning would exercise influence whenever an individual reads the text.[9] A new reality is created, experienced by the reader, when the different parts of the text are juxtaposed.

The prologue depicts pious Job. He offers sacrifice for his children in fear that they may have cursed God in their hearts. He accepts the loss of his goods and family, without in any way disparaging the majesty of God whom he recognizes has stripped him of his good fortune. He continues to worship this God, engaging in acceptable cultic responses to his loss.[10] Bereft of his property and family, he tears his garment, shaves his head, falls on the ground, and worships. Following the profound attack upon his health, and the complete removal of his social standing in the community, he manages to remain silent.[11] He rebukes his wife for suggesting that he act otherwise. Job responds correctly to his affliction. The prologue depicts as piety an exemplary person, accepting his or her lot in life, without complaint, without bitterness and above all, without questioning the accepted notions of God handed down by the magisterium. The piety of the prologue affirms the truth of theological formulations regardless of the reality of human experience. The narrator concludes that Job did not sin with his mouth.[12]

This is not, however, the only way that the prologue comments upon piety. When a text debunks a particular societal notion of piety, it attacks the very structures of that society. Most traditional Israelite formulations affirm that God rewards piety, and society acknowledges the perceived pious individual with approval and high social standing.[13] The prologue, however, introduces a notion of a piety that is *misunderstood* by the community. Legendary Job protests the traditional ideological consensus, thus creating the possibility of genuine piety that results in terrible affliction and the rejection of the community. This dramatically brings to question the traditional formulations.

By presenting an individual who was by definition pious, and yet afflicted, the text moved towards the reintegration of a whole underclass of Israel. These were the poor and disenfranchised, considered by established theologians during the time of the united monarchy to be afflicted by God as a result of their sins. The prologue attacked the smugness of the ruling classes who saw in their power and prosperity evidence of God's approval.

Notions of piety can be instruments of control, or, if wrested from the ruling powers, tremendous instruments of liberation. In the guise of a tract in support of traditional piety, the prologue in fact attacks its fundamental premise: that piety results in immediate and sure reward.

Clearly, the writer is not mocking Job, who desperately seeks to find his center in the worship of God. But by depicting such piety, the writer conceals a more profound questioning of the goodness of a god who would inflict such damage on a faithful worshipper. The reader's attention moves beyond an admiration of the faithful Job to a fundamental questioning of a religion that would require him to behave in such a manner.[14] Consequently, although Job's actions are not questioned in the narrative, they are deconstructed by the occasion that inspired them. The center of Job opens up these issues.

In the prologue, Job maintains his integrity and his piety by refusing to blaspheme God with his lips,[15] but the definition of integrity shifts in Job's dialogues.[16] Various definitions strive against each other, representing degrees of loyalty to one's religious convictions, to one's humanness, one's personality, one's experience. Job's wife sees integrity as an unwillingness to verbally curse God (2:9). The opposite of this integrity is understood therefore as one's uttering such a curse. The concept of integrity, common to both parts, links the prologue to the center.[17]

The word "integrity" is used in the text: *tûmah* (2:3, 2:9).[18] It occurs also in Proverbs 11:1-3:

> False scales are an abomination to the LORD;
> An honest weight pleases Him.
> When arrogance appears, disgrace follows,
> But wisdom is with those who are unassuming.
> The *integrity* of the upright guides them;
> The deviousness of the treacherous leads them to ruin.

Job 27:3-5 states:

> As long as there is life in me,
> And God's breath is in my nostrils,
> My lips will speak no wrong,
> Nor my tongue utter deceit.
> Far be it from me to say you are right;
> Until I die I will maintain my *integrity*.

And in 31:5-6:

> Have I walked with worthless men,
> Or my feet hurried to deceit?
> Let Him weigh me on the scale of righteousness;
> let God ascertain my *integrity*.

Integrity in Job concerns honest speech.[19] In Proverbs it is contrasted with "the crookedness of the treacherous," a context that implies such honesty. The term therefore depicts the truth for oneself and truth for God as being the same thing. But what if it is not honest to restrain one's curses of God? The word shifts in this way in the central portion of Job. Now integrity is held *against* God; integrity means asserting one's innocence, not God's innocence. In the frame Job is on trial, and to maintain his integrity he must not curse God. In the center God is on trial, and for Job to maintain his integrity, he must continue to assert his innocence, and God's guilt .[20]

In the center, integrity implies a distance from God. Job will defend his integrity against God's accusations. Job perceives that God opposes his integrity. This clearly does not accord with the normal standards of pious behavior, but rather constitutes a new definition of piety.

Although in the prologue Job did not sin against God with his lips (remaining silent), the center introduces us to Job who (in contrast) begins by opening his mouth.[21] The Job of the dialogues responds to the offense committed by the God of the prologue. He blasphemes; he sins against God with his lips (Robertson 1977:36).[22]

Job curses his life in the awareness that it is God who gives life.[23] He accuses God of tormenting him ruthlessly and without cause. The Deity is thereby described as cruel and demonic.[24] He dares God to kill him; pleads with God to leave him alone. He accuses God of injustice, of attending to him for the purpose of doing him harm.[25] God, the source of evil and disaster in the world, will not hear his cry, even though his cause is just. Job says that God takes pleasure in the suffering of innocent people.[26]

Job fancies himself a Titan, opposer of God's majesty. He appeals for some powerful blood avenger to secure justice for himself against God (Job 19:25, Good 1973:477).[27] He describes himself as one of God's mythical opponents, and challenges God to appear. He will greet him as a prince who welcomes an equal (Job 7:12; 31:37; Terrien 1954:899).[28]

Although Job will say none of these things in God's presence (as Satan had predicted), nor does he put the words "curse" and "God" in the same sentence, his characterizations are sufficiently accusatory, and may be designated as "sinning against God with his lips," as "cursing God." They stand in marked contrast to the pious pronouncements and the silence of Job in the prologue.[29]

The Joban center attacks a primary theological notion, the unwillingness to blaspheme. The center is crying out for the right to blaspheme in a situation where blasphemy might be the only appropriate response. In the frame cursing God is prohibited regardless of the circumstances, whereas in the center blasphemy might be appropriate in certain circumscribed formulations.[30]

The Joban dialogues debunk the notion that blasphemy is to be avoided and God is to be honored under all circumstances. The term piety is no longer functional in this part of the book. Rather, integrity, here referring to a reflective awareness of the reality of personal experience, is the absolute ideal for which Job is striving. Yahweh's speeches, on the other hand, seek to return to the notions of piety found in the prologue. God is to be trusted in spite of the breakdown of the relationship between virtue and reward.

Although Job claims no overt social implications for his contention with God (it was purely a personal action), clearly the friends see social implications.[31] If there is a potential situation in which the only rational thing to do is to forsake the (traditional) notions of integrity (piety) and to curse God, the entire social order will be brought into question. In response, they attack Job without mercy.

Yahweh's speeches, although much more *in the style* of the center, find their sentiments *in the spirit* of the prologue, by depicting an insecure God anxious to demonstrate his accomplishments to his underlings.[32] It makes perfect narrative sense to have the God of the prologue speak as he does in the speeches. He blusters and bullies Job, never effectively answering Job's questions.[33] Such a God, Job seems to say, deserves to be blasphemed.

The epilogue, however, is highly ambiguous. It does double duty in a holistic reading of the book. On the one hand, Yahweh's approval of Job reflects Job's pious activities in the prologue; but on the other hand, it affirms the blasphemous statements made in the center.[34] Job returns to quiet and trustful piety in the epilogue,[35] but by following the center, the epilogue introduces many ironic and disharmonic elements. These elements transform the understanding of God and of Job. One might therefore read the ending as a vindication of Job by looking to the theophany (and Job's survival of Yahweh's appearance) and his restoration; or as a vindication of Yahweh's justice, attending to Job's blasphemous speeches and his abject repentance. Job actually says nothing in the epilogue. He is dramatically depicted only from the outside, with no insight into his internal reactions. Job's correct response to Yahweh's rebuke becomes the cause of Job's restoration.

Job therefore disperses into many stories, each occupying the same 42 chapters.[36] Two of the most prominent are the story of pious Job and the story of rebellious Job.[37] These stories use some of the same textual features, and studiously avoid any serious attention to contentious passages.

In the story of pious Job, the Satan desires to test Job's perfection and sends terrible suffering upon him. Job responds with worship and pious statements, and then finally silence under great provocation. He proceeds to defend his innocence against the false accusations of his friends. The speeches of Yahweh trouble this story, and are either ignored or subjected to tortuous interpretations. Yahweh, we are told, rebukes Job for the beginnings of doubt. Some interpreters distinguish between the perfect piety of the prologue, and the lapses subsequent to that point—Yahweh is only rebuking his later faults while Job remains pure in the most essential qualities. Finally, because of his overall faithfulness despite a momentary lapse, God restores and vindicates Job. With closure accomplished, the implied reader[38] relaxes and is satisfied that virtue is rewarded and sin punished.

In the story of rebellious Job, Job goes to such extremes to maintain his piety that he renders himself ridiculous and irrelevant. God's willingness to afflict Job displays either his wanton cruelty, or perhaps his inscrutability. Job explodes in righteous rage against the unfairness of his position. God tries to bully him into submission through a declaration of his power. God so humiliates Job that he pleads for mercy, and concedes everything.[39] Finally, God restores and vindicates Job, but ultimately damns himself to complete irrelevance.

Without more direct evidence, the interpreter may only imagine the historical events behind these conflicting readings. Certainly the period of post-exilic Israel fits many of the features of this dissonant text.[40] Israel was in the process of transforming the character of its religion, manipulating its symbols in more radical ways than ever before. The Israelite religion was transformed into what is subsequently called Judaism.

There were those in Israel who longed for the previous simplicity of a nostalgically remembered Yahwism, either of the ancestral or early monarchic periods.[41] Some could not accept the oncoming Jewish sensibilities but saw the bankruptcy of the ancient Yahwism as imported from Babylon. They were centrally responsible for the extant book of Job and the radically negative picture of Yahweh.

Finally, the concurrent interpreters of Jewish tradition (represented by the friends) opposed most dramatically the rebellious reading. The mysterious disruption of the third cycle of speeches may stand as mute reminder that the ultimate expression of this rejection of deity was ruthlessly suppressed. Job never curses God without qualification in the extant text.

The text exposes these ideological functions of society. First the idea of socially approved behavior (Job's behavior) is separated from the concept of societal recognition. Then the notion of piety is demolished altogether and replaced by integrity; a new kind of integrity not concerned with faithful adherence to the religious taboos (blasphemy) but rather concerned with a person's loyalty towards his or her own experience.

Job remains a sympathetic figure throughout; a model of whatever kind of behavior the tradent deemed honorable. There is, however, a deep-seated confusion as to who is Job. This points to a conflict regarding the definition of socially admirable behavior, the presumed historical context that produced the dissonance. The dominant group supported the behavior that would uphold the social structure (the law of retribution), but the social structures themselves were breaking down. Whether the conflict raged between priest and sage, or between sage and sage, it represented a wider societal reorganization.

GOD'S APPROVAL AND DISAPPROVAL OF JOB

The narrative of the prologue hinges upon God's approval of Job and of his activities. Three times the narrator affirms Job's righteousness, and twice God repeats the approbation. The text describes Job as an individual who fears God and avoids evil, perfect and upright,[42] the greatest in the East.[43]

Yahweh repeats this praise twice in the divine council. The narrator describes Job's activities following his affliction as without taint of sin. After the first trial Job "did not ascribe unworthiness to God." After the second, as seen, he "did not sin with his lips." There would seem to be a progression between the first narrative comment and the second. The narrowing of the scope of Job's sinlessness points to an internal struggle in Job, whereby he might have sinned in his heart, although not with his lips.

God is most noted by his absence in the poetic dialogues that make up the bulk of Job. Clearly Job's friends feel strongly that God disapproves of Job and they argue against Job's protestations of innocence. Their speeches are preoccupied with persuading Job of his guilt and explaining to him how he may return to God's good graces. If Job is good, God will give him things.

Job's position is more ambiguous. He shares with his friends the basic retributive position that God must disapprove of him as evidenced by his affliction. He insists not that God approves of him but rather that God's attitude and subsequent actions appear unjust. He has expected to earn God's approval, and its notable absence is a mystery to him.

The book of Job resembles a trial or a test; but, as Vogels asks, who is on trial, God or Job? (1980:835). The prologue describes a test of Job's piety initiated by the Satan, assented to by Yahweh. "If you attack his property he will curse you to your face!" (1:11)

Job in the center accuses God of many things, putting Yahweh on the defensive. Job's friends defend God, and then Yahweh defends himself. Job places God on trial, questioning his justice, his moral governance of the world. Does God know what he is doing? Has he treated his servant fairly? Job accuses God and appeals for justice, finally compelling God to answer the charges by means of a solemn curse formula (ch. 31).

Supposedly, Job's perplexity (unaided by the friends' efforts) will be resolved by the appearance of Yahweh. Yahweh, when he appears, does indeed express strong disapproval of Job's statements, Job's hubris in daring to question God. This does not, however, solve the dilemma presented by the narrative. Yahweh does not address Job's original question, why he was afflicted, but only his effrontery to impugn God's wisdom in governing the world. One might even wonder whether such a God, who bullies, blusters, and overpowers a human questioner is worthy of the respect offered him (Robertson 1977:48-49); whether gaining the approval of such a god should be important to a person of integrity.

Yahweh, by his two speeches, seeks again to put Job on trial, by attacking not his integrity (the point of challenge in the prologue) but rather his right to impugn God's justice. Yahweh attempts to shift the basis upon which the entire argument of the book has been developed. His attack is *ad hominem*, never addressing any of the issues that have been raised previously. Whereas the sympathies had formerly rested with Job throughout the prologue and the dialogues, Yahweh's speeches seek sympathy for the much-maligned deity whose power and majesty have been unfairly attacked by Job (Robertson 1977:48-49).

Of course, Yahweh is a character in the story, and one must wonder if a reader's sympathies do indeed shift as a result of Yahweh's defense of his *droit de seigneur?* The placement of the speeches in the midst of the entire book affects the expression of sympathy. Yahweh's comments taken by themselves are not inconsistent with many other pronouncements of God's

majesty in which they are taken very seriously and sympatheti-
cally (e.g. Isaiah 40).

But in Job the reader's sympathies are with the main character throughout both previous sections; the Job who suffers
and the Job who complains have both elicited solicitous concern. Accused by the Satan, afflicted by God and accosted by
the friends, Job remains the hero.

Yahweh's speeches therefore represent not Job's answer but
the final desolation and abandonment of Job, the failure of his
last hope for redress.[44] Job is attacked ruthlessly from the very
quarter where he hoped (against expectation) that he would be
granted explanation and perhaps recompense. Yahweh longs
for the silent Job of the prologue, rather than the blasphemous
Job of the center. Are the readers thereby compelled to add to
Job the final blow? They do not abandon him, as does his God,
his wife, and his friends. Rather, they feel the depth of Job's
sadness and his fear. His response of submission, admittedly
ambiguous, is not the final resolution of the problem.

By not attacking the integrity of Job, but rather by defending his own integrity, God accepts Job's definition of the problem. God declares that his chief concern remains to preserve his
own innocence at the expense of Job's. The reader mourns with
Job as he cowers before a superior power.

In this context, Yahweh's stunning reversal in the epilogue
must be understood. Much controversy remains as to the exact
nature of Job's responses to Yahweh's speeches in 40:4-5 and
particularly 42:6. Some have seen them as an abject repentance and recantation of all that had been said previously.[45]
Others, particularly Dale Patrick (1979:278),[46] have noted
various degrees of rebellion in these statements; some even
remark at a flat mockery and rejection of Yahweh's authority
and majesty. Why the ambiguity? Perhaps there are linguistic
usages inaccessible to modern interpreters. Perhaps the text was
damaged or distorted through the process of transmission. Or
one might, with Patrick and others, claim that the rebellious
meaning is plain, but theologians wish to avoid its implications.
At the very least, these statements of Job are intrinsically ambig-

uous, and because of the unusual vocabulary and syntax, they may be read either way. No final adjudication is possible.

The epilogue addresses the matter from an entirely different perspective, one that throws the whole problem into disarray. The God of the epilogue once again characterizes Job's speech with glowing words of approval: [addressing the friends] "For you have not spoken the truth about Me as did My servant Job."[47] The seemingly ludicrous line now follows Yahweh's blistering attack on the words of Job, and the tearful recantation of Job's words, and throws the entire discussion into narrative confusion.[48] Polzin (1974:186) observes with a touch of irony:

> God apparently acts like the kind of person he praises Job for denying him to be. Concerning Job's friends, at the same time as he says they are wrong in their naive insistence that he always punishes evil, he threatens to punish them for being evil. He will avert disaster from them if they repent and admit that he does not always avert disaster from the repentant.

One may posit stylistic carelessness to explain this glaring contradiction in God's approval of Job, but the central knot has not thereby been removed, only displaced. One must still justify why this carelessness was allowed to remain through many phases of editing. Job has been written thus and readers so read it. This feature of dissonance powerfully opens some of the central ideological conflicts in the text.[49]

The traditional view of piety is bifurcated. The piety demanded by the God of the prologue and the speeches of Yahweh conforms to the traditional theological framework of Israel, but Job's painful exclamations in the center gain the approval of Yahweh in the epilogue. Notions of piety are reversed: the Job of the center becomes the pious figure of whom God approves; the Job of the prologue, a hopeless sycophant.

A new picture of God is created, one that approves of Job's blasphemy. Thus are forged alliances within the text that run counter to the historical explanation of transmission (noted in chapter 2). Conflicting pictures of God and Job are created that do not correspond to the two parts of Job historically explained, but rather develop along the lines of narrative formation as it takes place in the newly ordered text. The intention of the author might or might not play a significant role in this juxtaposition, but social consciousness and the ideological struggles of Israelite society certainly do.

If a single, clear ideological picture were dominant, the end result would have been a more harmonious text. The fact that the tradents did not have total authority to transform the text into the image of their own ideological picture indicates the presence of serious political struggle.

As the text stands, the implicit reader's sympathy for Job has remained consistent throughout the various portions of the story. "Job so gives voice to our own fears, doubts, and frustrations that we cannot help but sympathize with him" (Robertson 1977:37). Even the deity finally sympathizes with Job, when he approves of Job's words and vindicates him before his community. In so doing, God disassembles his own arguments, and shows himself to be in competition with Job's friends for characterization as the least sympathetic figure in the narrative. God's feeble attempts to rebuild Job's shattered life seem by their very shallowness and insensitivity to prove the soundness of Job's accusations.[50]

Job has maintained his integrity and Yahweh has lost his. How then did the various Israelite societies read this text in the light of this conflict? The positions regarding God's approval or disapproval of Job do not split off into successive readings, as did those that originated from the issue of Job's piety. The entire conflict rather hinges on the interpretation of 42:7, the beginning of the epilogue: "You have not spoken truly of me, but Job my servant has." Of which behavior did God approve; the piety of the prologue or the rebellion of the center (Driver 1921:lix)? (It would be narratively absurd to interpret Yahweh's words as referring to Job's words of repentence.) Which expresses God's evaluation of Job, the speeches of Yahweh (chs. 38-41) or Yahweh's statement in 42:7? These questions cannot be answered in the extant Job. This lack speaks of the dramatic failure of consensus concerning the conceptualization of God.

The historical events in Israel elucidate some of the dissonantal features of the text. A breakdown in the concepts of transcendence occurs in that small nation. There no longer exists a certainty that God establishes and maintains the social and cosmic order. The text suggests that God in fact attacks the social order, and introduces chaos into the system. If God were to approve of a rebel, then rebellion is sanctioned, social order threatened.[51] Persons no longer express confidence in their knowledge of God's will; the divine symbols have been drained of their power and authority. Cultic institutions lose their influence and their ability to interpret historical events. The disruption questions the possibility of any ultimately authoritative value system, which in turn undermines the very myths that uphold the superstructure of a particular society.

What then is the book of Job about? Or with what do the various component pieces of Job concern themselves? Is there any particular theme that gains dominance in the struggle of ideas that the book embodies? Dissonance asserts itself not only between the piety and rebellion of Job, or between the approval and disapproval of God, but between both, for the two dissonantal flashpoints interact with each other. God both approves and disapproves of the piety and the blasphemy of Job. Dissonance is thereby expressed between these two loci, producing a new form of thematic dissonance. One does not decide which tension truly describes Job, but rather how the different interpretive difficulties interact.

Fault lines not only cut through the attempted resolutions of Job's fundamental issues, but more to the very heart of the text, the problems themselves begin to break down. Job as it stands does not answer the questions. They are raised, clarified, magnified, but never answered. The questions themselves are questioned. The multitudes of answers cancel each other out. This closely corresponds to the historical period in Israel's history when their symbolic system (theology and cult) began to crumble at its foundation.

THE ABSENCE OF THE SATAN

Readers find themselves in a privileged position regarding the action in the Joban prologue (Whedbee 1977:7). Job and his friends believe that all human experience proceeds from God's hand. The reader is, however, informed that the reality is considerably more complex. The narrative introduces the figure of the Satan as a major participant in the action which results in Job's affliction. Job and his friends know nothing of this.

The Satan is a considerably complex figure himself, and his role has been variously interpreted. He is neither the faithful servant of God, an undifferentiated member of the heavenly host, nor the declared enemy of God and all goodness in the world. He travels throughout the earth, ostensibly to test the piety of humans, and when God draws his attention to Job, the Satan immediately questions Job's integrity.

Officially, he appears as a loyal servant and counselor, responding to God's initiation in the discussion of Job's piety.[52] However, upon closer examination the Satan seems in control of the dialogue with his lord.[53] His hostility towards Yahweh and towards Yahweh's prized servant is barely concealed. His contempt for Yahweh's judgments lies just below the surface, and the ease with which he manipulates God to do *his* will is a marvel of subtlety.[54]

The heavenly narrative therefore acquits God of venality, but only by robbing him of his wisdom and power. The wisdom and power all belong to the Satan. The Satan questions Yahweh's generous praise of Job and suggests a test that would enable his accusations to be verified. He (not Yahweh) is the direct cause of Job's troubles and seems to manipulate Yahweh for his own (albeit obscure) purposes. Upon completion of the first test (the destruction of Job's family and property) Yahweh accuses the Satan of inciting him to afflict Job without cause (*hinnam*), thus implying that the Satan compelled Yahweh to afflict Job contrary to the divine nature (Weiss 1983:37).

In 1:11 the Satan says "But lay *your* hand. . . " but Yahweh is quoted in 1:12, referring to Job, "all that is his is in *your* power (literally 'hand')," thus evading his responsibility. In 1:16 there is a contrast between the hand of the Satan and the hand of Yahweh. Yahweh insists that the Satan should strike Job. Yahweh will not do it himself (1:12), and the narrator duly tells us what happened without making direct reference to the causative agent. The context, however, clearly points to the

Satan, the one who has just been sent from the council with a specific divine commission. Finally, the Satan challenges Yahweh again, "but lay a hand (literally 'your hand') on his bones and flesh . . . " (2:5), but Job 2:7 states that the Satan left the Lord's presence and he (the Satan is the immediate antecedent) struck Job.[55]

From the perspective of the prologue, it would seem that the Satan was bested. Being afflicted in the most grievous fashion imaginable, Job remained steadfast. However, Job perceived that it was God who tormented him. One would thereby expect a final scene between the Satan and Yahweh, where the Satan would concede the argument (Tur-Sinai 1967:36). Instead there is only absence.

Attempts at explanations for this absence abound. Snaith (1968:17) contends that the Satan has been defeated and there is therefore no more need for him to show his face. For Vawter (1983:30), the Satan is only an agent of God and thus of no importance. Habel (1985:81) believes that he has been replaced by Job's wife and friends. These various literary and theological explanations beg the question. As an important actor in the beginning scenes, some resolution is needed. It is missing.

The Satan is absent from the dialogues between Job and his friends. Neither Job nor his friends consider a personal alternative to God who might bear some responsibility for Job's torment.[56] One would expect that Yahweh would blame the Satan in his own speeches, as he had in 2:3. Instead, regarding the Satan, there is only silence.

The epilogue is the stylistic companion to the prologue and one would therefore look for the reappearance of the Satan. Instead, in the concluding portion of the frame narrative there is no further mention of this figure. The naive wrapping up of loose ends, whereby Job's property and even his children are restored, makes no mention of the wager. Instead, the text completely ignores the Satan after he afflicts Job with a disfiguring disease. Neither acknowledged nor referred to, this major figure seems forgotten. The human desire for closure grasps for some explanation of this absence. Again, narrative explanations abound, but they are strained beyond the breaking point.

There exists therefore a confusion of responsibility in the very structure of Job. The language clouds the decisive moral tone that most readers want to find in the book. Historically this confusion could be the result of an attempt, at a later transmissional period, to protect Yahweh's reputation.[57] By shifting some of the blame to a distinctly different personage, God escapes relatively unscathed.[58]

The attempted obfuscation is not successful, since many aspects of God's responsibility remain in the text, for without the direct activity of God the story would discard one of its major threads and lose the reader's interest. Human relationship with God is paramount here, not the activity of the Satan. The reader is told that "fire of God fell from heaven," (1:16),[59] and a great *ruah* (here meaning wind, but also the word for spirit) struck down the greater part of Job's life.[60] Also, it is God's hand that must do the deed in the Satan's haunting comments. The Satan figure, by having served his function, is dropped from the rest of the story.

This jarring absence may demonstrate that the Satan myth made an incomplete conquest of the imaginations of the Israelites. They were in a transition from an ethos that blamed (and credited) everything to God, to one that (because rival powers did not threaten them) allowed the Satan to do most of the supernatural dirty work. Even in the Persian period, many were still uncomfortable with so reducing the majesty of Yahweh by placing things outside of his control.

Does the absence of the Satan figure do any more than reflect the ambiguity that the Israelites felt concerning this rival force? Why then is the Satan painted with so much power? If not nicer than Yahweh, he is certainly presented as smarter, more in control. The fact that he is not penciled in at the end of the book, or even in its middle, indicates a possible disdain and avoidance of the implications that are resident in such a symbol. The continuing presence of the Satan would have disturbed the fabric of the book, changing its focus, which is squarely upon the behavior of Yahweh.

The Satan's absence cannot be explained by his lack of importance, by subsuming him into the activity of God, or because his role has been replaced by earthly characters in their proper sphere.[61] The Satan would thereby become *de facto* the agent of an omnipotent God with no independent will or existence of his own.[62] An examination of the text will not allow such a construction. The Satan does indeed fulfill the role of God's agent, but in fact his independence and his superiority are highlighted by the narrative, emphasized by the words of Yahweh himself, "*You have incited* me against him to destroy him for no good reason; to ruin him needlessly (*hinnam*)."[63]

Clearly, the Satan suggests the action, persuades God of its advisability, and brings it to pass.[64] He cannot be seen as unimportant. The only action God initiates is the initial exposure of Job's behavior to the heavenly court's consideration.

The Satan absorbs the hostility that would have been directed at Yahweh, but by doing so, transforms Yahweh into a "buffoon" (Kinet 1983:31). He thereby compromises the primacy and uniqueness of Yahweh.[65]

The glaring absence of the figure in the book's final three sections opens up the interpretations of Job to divergent possibilities.[66] With this (the *most*?) significant factor omitted from the final considerations of all the other main characters, all conclusions (the conclusion of Yahweh's speeches and the conclusion of the epilogue) are thereby thrown into question.

The Satan's troubling absence corresponds to a disturbing lack of answers to any of the book's questions. Divine operations are completely hidden from the earthly participants, to whom Yahweh is the only active agent. Had Job and his friends only known the events in heaven, their arguments would have appeared irrelevant, as they do to the omniscient reader. The issue should not have remained, why did God afflict Job, but rather, who will be bested in this supernatural wager?[67] Knowing about the Satan would have made Job angrier at God. Knowledge of the Satan would not have answered any of Job's questions; Job would inevitably have raised new ones.

The Satan's activity in the prologue undermines the validity of all the assumptions of Job and his friends in the center. The lack of any resolution with the Satan parallels the disquiet felt at the conclusion of a careful reading of Job, and leads one to speculate that this unease exemplifies some of the actual concerns of the book. All connections in Job turn back upon themselves and remain unresolved. The book is left hanging in midair. Job depicts the unease felt in a society where ideology and experience have fallen into open combat, where people have become deeply disillusioned with all the supposed answers of the past, and know of no new ones adequate for the current historical situation.[68]

ACCOUNTING FOR THE DISSONANCE

Dissonance must be explained both in terms of historical Israel and critical theory. The societal picture of the political groups in Israel that produced this dissonant text will be explored in the final chapter. A few hermeneutical remarks are in order here.

Three hermeneutical stances serve to highlight the dissonant features of the text. Chapter 2 explored the *historical dissonance*; the struggles between the different sections of Job which were produced by the act of inserting a poetic and reflective center into the heart of legendary Job, the two works representing two different eras in Israelite sapiential thought. Historical dissonance occurs in the gross structures of the extant Job, neatly divided into the frame and the center.

By generating an entirely new product, the various parts and features are transformed into a unique and novel juxtaposition, thus illustrating *structural dissonance*. Through this juxtaposition, parts which meant one thing in the historically distinct sections come to mean something different. Other crucial passages are consequently ignored, sacrificed to the enforced harmonization of a particular reading.

When this process is seen from the perspective of the reader's expectations, as determined by their respective hermeneutic communities, one finds dissonance in reading. Different hermeneutic groups construe the same passage in entirely different ways. The suppression of rival readings never succeeds completely. Alternative renderings remain as ideological ghosts, both building up and tearing down the privileged reading.[69]

4

THE
BOOK OF JOB
IN THE
WORLD

THE HERMENEUTICAL SIGNIFICANCE
OF DISSONANCE

The dissonantal features in Job juxtapose various hermeneutical readings in the same text so that they signify different books. The discussion of *historical dissonance* dominates most of the Joban scholarly discourse. In this genetic reading, i.e. reading concerned with the genesis of the text (Sternberg 1987:13-16), the interpreter must construe the story of Job as an artifact offering clues for reconstructing the historical events that formed it. The "story" is actually the story of Job's genesis, development, and transmission. Occurrences of dissonance then suggest sites of textual activity and provide historical information for the genetic reading. Chapter 2 of the present study tells this story.

Historical dissonance explains a text through events in the history of the people that produced the material. In the book of Job, the critic explores the source of the frame and center in terms of different periods of Israelite history.

Structural dissonance (whose object corresponds to but is not limited by formalist concerns) sees the story of Job as the struggle for dominance among readings, and acknowledges the book's failure to resolve the issues it raises in being read. The damaged, lopsided narrative generated by the relationship between parts of the fixed text constitutes the structural story. This transforms the interpretation of smaller, historically determined sections. The whole seen as a juxtaposition of disparate parts creates a new reality in the text's final form.

Such a reading brackets or ignores the issue of the text's history by examining the surface features that divide the text into parts and by exploring how those parts interact in the reading in a mixture of conflictive and harmonic impulses. In the book of Job, comparisons among the prologue, the Joban dialogues, the speeches of Yahweh and the epilogue highlight points of conflict between the sections.

The dissonantal reading is difficult to distinguish from the dissonantal *text* (structural dissonance). They might be in fact two aspects of the same phenomenon. The reading, however, notes how consumers of the material construe a text, conforming it to their expectations. The reader must skillfully weave various features into a previously nonexistent narrative whole, selectively ignoring those features that conflict with the imposed narrative structure.

The text, of course, resists arbitrary readings, and the tensive relationship between the attempted reading and its level of failure constitutes the dissonantal reading. The story of how an implied reader might encounter the fixed text constitutes the third reading. In the book of Job, the particular attempts to impose readings collide with the concrete nature of the text. Chapter 3 of this study told the structural story and the reader's story from this dissonantal perspective.

It remains now to approach the text and to produce a contemporary reading by borrowing from these three perspectives. I will here create a broad-ranging dissonantal reading, one that sees the feature of dissonance as a crucial key to understanding the phenomena of Job. Hence, the question addressed in this chapter is: How does Job, seen as a dissonantal text, interact with the external, non-textual world?

By "world," I mean not only the world through which the text of Job passed historically, but also the various contemporary communities to which Job might speak, including our own. The following discussion constitutes the recreation of the textual event, which will include both a discussion of the moments of Job's crystallization, but also its subsequent reception and absorption by various communities.

When the text itself could no longer be transformed, the tradents well into the Middle Ages added marginal readings developing a contrast between the actual words and letters of the text, and the way a text *should* be read. A community's power to change the text receded only gradually.

By examining the impact various communities exerted on the text of Job, one might be able to picture the ideology of the literary mentality in a particular period of time, in this case, post-exilic Israel. Not producing an exact reflection, however, the text appears as a distorted or reactive view of what was (and is) going on in the world as it passes through. The text also speaks to and changes its various environments.

Most pre-modern interpreters of Job interpret the book as an exhortation to patient, noncomplaining piety. This reading points to no particular time but to a societal group with a stake in supporting the institutional superstructure and the values of non-resistance. Likewise, the skeptical reading reflects, however imperfectly, a time when profound values are questioned.

JOB AND THE POST-EXILIC WORLD OF ISRAEL

The place of dissonance in a literary work transports the interpreter to the deep-seated conflicts forming and informing the text's crystallization. The pain experienced in reading conjoins with the "historical" turmoil surrounding the text. The non-textual conflict that produced Job in its final form occurred in Israelite society during a time of significant and radical change. Different possible sources may be found for the same dissonantal features. Conflicts between two hermeneutical factions, one dominant and one subservient, often took the form of overt political opposition, but could also have been more subtle and subversive. There exists within Job both a radical challenge to the societal mores and a vehement defense of those same moral and political positions.

It is sometimes difficult to tell which view takes possession of a particular passage. In modern times the more radical readings tend to stand out, mentioning as they do, the unmentionable corners of theology. Such readings hold strong appeal in a world where the moral props of society have broken down. However, the pious reading has been more influential, reinforced in most faith communities for obvious reasons.

The tracks of these conflicts are hidden by the successive editorial layering, which must be peeled away to reveal the central disharmonic impulses of the text. An examination of the seams and fissures of the text offers a key to rediscovering these historical features.

What follows is an imaginative reconstruction of the historical world that produced Job, an attempt to correlate the conflicts of Job with what is known of ancient Israel. There are many correspondences, but the connections are tentative because this historical reading is necessarily *imposed* upon a text that continues to resist historical categorization.

A Deuteronomistic impulse shaped much of the Hebrew Bible, insisting that the histories of nations were intrinsically linked to their moral and spiritual character. Yahweh would punish evil nations and reward good ones. Three groups in Israel adapted the Deuteronomistic position to their own unique literary requirements. The priests employed the cult to reenact in ritual their affirmation of a faithful and consistent God who was joined to Israel in covenantal relationship. They dominated the teaching institutions that rose up around the second Temple. They enclosed God and created public, human access to the holy. The prophets through their dramatic rhetoric and popular following adapted Deuteronomistic belief by declaring that God would punish Israel for its sins, or had already.

The bureaucrats, who were the sages, by their ability to manipulate the various governmental institutions, had a vested interest in the Deuteronomistic theology which served as propaganda for their form of government. The governmental structure was patterned on the heavenly court. It was thought that the concepts of justice and righteousness were shared by human and celestial leaders. Many of the sages argued for this position on the basis of their own moral observations.

At some point, Israelite theologians individualized the Deuteronomistic doctrine, applying it to particular members of the community rather than to the group as a whole. This individualization might have occurred either at the same time as the early Deuteronomistic promulgation, or perhaps as the result of a later period of intellectual development. Crenshaw (1980:11) notes that such individual responsibility encouraged the development of skepticism by emphasizing human corruption.

This Deuteronomistic impulse came under attack in Israel as a result of national experience—political reality transformed the theological reality. Various nations subjugated Israel during the post-exilic period, and individual Israelites suffered extreme want at the hands of many occupying forces. In reaction to the disparity between the theological picture given and the historical experience of Israel, there arose prophets and sages who radically questioned this interpretive scheme.[1]

These various groups struggled for control of the legendary material about Job, both through additions, editing techniques, and enforced readings. Three positions can be isolated within Job, regarding this proposed "law" of retribution. Some rejected it entirely, some held to it with reservations, and others held to it strictly. *All these positions are represented in Job*, both by the individual speeches, and the relationships between the speeches and other sections. As discussed earlier, a single pericope can function within all three readings, with various textual and narrative elements shifting from the foreground to the background and then in reverse.

No reading of Job fully dominates the others. As a result, the modern historical inquirer finds it difficult if not impossible to determine precisely which political or social group performed the final redaction of the text.[2] On the contrary, the text resists the attempt to identify it with any particular group. Perhaps one of the redacting groups concealed its influence because of the revolutionary nature of its positions. Hiding their radical pronouncements in relatively innocent (or at least defused) surroundings, this group concealed its identity.

Further difficulties confront the interpreter endeavoring to correctly identify historical traces in the literature of Israel. It is likely that later tradents beyond the point of the text's fixity, tampered with written material. Spivak (1976:lxxvi) quotes Freud: "[There are] various methods . . . for making [an undesirable] book innocuous. [1] Offending passages . . . [are] made illegible . . . The next copyist would produce a text . . . which had gaps. [2] Another way would be . . . to proceed to distort the text. [3] Best of all, the whole passage would be erased and a new one which said exactly the opposite put in its place."

Although their impulses were more conservative regarding Israelite institutions, these later tradents had to respect the story's fundamental structure even when it undermined those institutions. As a result, they did not fully eradicate Job's initial message. They tried to combat the liberating influence of Job by strictly enforced readings of the text, readings that have now taken on a life of their own. These readings were not consciously composed to combat a perceived menace. Rather they developed in response to societal and existential fears and pressures experienced by the final transmitting group.

A contemporary reading must begin with a diachronic discussion that looks upon dissonance from the perspective of its activity within time (historical dissonance). This approach must bracket the issue of the interpreter's stance as participant and assume a certain measure of heuristic objectivity. The postexilic period is the time of most intense literary activity in the formation of the book of Job. Job encompasses the conflict between conserving and radical influences at that time, perhaps between groups (priest and sage, for instance) or within a group, most likely the sapiential community.[3]

The post-exilic period embodies a significant paradigm shift in Israelite history. In the political realm, the Israelite people were thinking the unthinkable: they no longer identified themselves as a nation but rather as a culturally and religiously constituted body. They reformed and recreated their institutions, adding to and subtracting from the traditional cultic formulations to account for the new reality confronting them. Their communities now spanned a wide geographical area as a result of the exile. They had to cope with their defeat and powerlessness at the hands of various colonial powers. Enforced pluralism became the dominant reality. Out of this milieu, the various tradents fixed the text of Job.

But Job cannot be dismissed so easily as the product of a single historical, albeit dissonantal moment. No reading dominates because of the text's ambiguous nature. Each reading contends with the others in turn. Different communities have interacted with the text in significantly intrusive ways. Although true of all texts, *many* different communities engaged Job in this manner. One does not explicate the story of Job by a mere snapshot taken at the time it gained fixity, or even by an account of its transmissional history up to that point.

Rather, the story continues as each group reforms the tradition, some through an actual reordering of the text through additions, subtractions and interpolations; others through enforced readings.[4] This makes the story of the book of Job open-ended. One can not properly distinguish between the text itself and the various cultural *uses* of the ancient narrative.[5]

A CONTEMPORARY READING OF JOB

Previous Readings of Job

The contemporary reading is synchronic. That is to say, Job is categorized by means of diverse readings without respect to the specific historical context of those readings (structural dissonance). The social situation of the various hermeneutic communities shall impinge on the discussion, but will not be the central focus. Rather, the various readings are reviewed from a topical standpoint and categorized in terms of their chief concerns.

Many readings contend for the soul of Job's story. In the history of interpretation, each reading has in turn been an attempted imposition of order onto a disparate text. The following is an attempt to read the work *as* a disparate text by using the dissonantal features as the source of interpretative information. Certainly, this too imposes a harmonizing impulse upon the text, but this impulse is held in check, and the disharmonic features are not suppressed.

Various harmonic readings have failed adequately to account for the text of Job.

Reading 1: Some readers understand the book of Job to be about a person's willingness to suffer and remain faithful to an inconsistent deity. This reading construes Job as a "pious example." One must not read Job in terms of its present form (one is told), but rather must reconstitute the original legendary tale. The issues raised in the dialogue are ignored, and the simple tale provides comfort to pious individuals. Many who subscribe to the "pious example" reading of Job engage in complex and refined textual analysis. One must not see this reading as necessarily simple-minded and superficial, but much subtlety is lost to the story when the pious Job is emphasized.

Reading 2: Many interpreters reject any possibility of engaging the entire book. They correctly note the book's confusion. One can only make sense of its separate parts, trying to reconstruct the development of the poetic narrative, focusing on a particular cluster of texts, declaring them the "true" Job (Glatzer 1969:11). Usually, this style of Joban interpretation highlights some part of the book as uniquely relevant to the whole of the human condition. For instance, an existentialist reading will center on the elusive or absent God and Job's distress at God's non-appearance in the center. Neo-orthodoxy will characterize Job as the "faithful sufferer." The liberal highlights Job as the questioner of institutional truth. Certain more recent interpretations would emphasize the psychological aspects of the drama. Each of these points resides in the text of Job, but none may be identified as the true or the definitive reading.

Reading 3: Others assert that the elements in Job do fit together according to some pre-existent though secret pattern. This pattern must be discovered and justified by cleverly putting together the pieces, as a jigsaw puzzle.

Reading 4: Yet still, other modern readings engage in a cynical rejection of all constructive theological pronouncements. They enlist Job in a complete repudiation of the established religious and social order.

The Dissonantal Reading

In contrast to the previous four readings, this author contends that the book of Job is "*about*" dissonance.[6] Robert Polzin

(1974:183) remarks, "Confrontation of inconsistencies appears to be as much a feature of the book's structure as of its content . . . these many inconsistencies are essential to its message." Dissonance is in fact the book's most prominent feature. All the other readings have in common some kind of struggle against the dissonance of the book. The disharmonic elements of the book of Job create a kind of whole; not in hopeless disarray, as some would claim, but neither as a coherent story.

As mentioned in the previous chapter, the final tradents before and after fixity intended Job to be read as a single piece, regardless of their diverse expectation as to *how* that might be accomplished. People naturally read it as a single work: a narrative whole which is some kind of account of the life of a man named Job. The reader, as the writer had done before, juxtaposes the different parts according to prearranged plan, creating an enforced structural unity. Therefore, a full literary study must in some way take account of the entire book, although the guiding principle for uniting the whole in this case would be a disparate one.

Those who interpret a text according to the paradigm of dissonance engage in high paradox. They must first embrace the dissonance as the chief hermeneutical construct which creates the literature. Then they must violate this construct by unifying the book under a single interpretive principle. Finally these critics must acknowledge that the text shall necessarily break free of the imposed structure. Such a process is unavoidable. The unifying and deconstructive impulses work in modulation.

The Benefits of a Dissonantal Reading of Job

This proposed reading claims that Job is indeed to be read as some sort of whole, and that dissonance is the primary feature of this whole, both formally and ideologically. Does such a stance elicit a fruitful response from the text of Job? In a pluralistic academic context, it is difficult to develop a useful set of criteria that enables the reader to choose between interpretations. Sallie McFague (1987:63, 79) has made some important suggestions concerning metaphor that may be applied to any interpretive task:

> [Does the work] have both marks of a good metaphor, both the shock and the *recognition*? Do these metaphors both disorient and reorient? Do they evoke a response of hearing something new and something interesting? Are they both disclosive and illuminating, both a revelation and in some sense true? . . . At the close of day, one asks which distortion (assuming that all pictures are false in some respects) is better, by asking what attitudes each encourages. This is not the first question to ask, but it may well be the last.

A dissonantal reading will note that first, Job does not effectively answer the questions raised by the text, which are the problem of the existence of disinterested piety, and the explanation of undeserved suffering. *There are in fact no answers in Job.* The various attempts at answering these critical human questions all neutralize each other. Raschke (1982:11) observes, "Every quantum of discourse cancels itself in the moment of 'expression.' It does not express anything except a 'space' between itself and what was said before."

In this ambiguity Job addresses the most perplexing aspects of human existence. Job's suffering remains unexplained, as does suffering in most of the world. Job searches for meaning and authentic experience, but finds no specific answers. The offered solutions seem to mock both Job and the reader.

Second, in this dissonantal reading, God remains a cloudy and ambiguous figure.[7] How big is God? Petty and small, or majestic and all-powerful? The operation of the heavenly council, the activity of Satan, and Job's search for a mediator all undermine the rigid monotheism of Israel, although nothing new is put in its place. Rather, certainty is overthrown; confusion and openness remain. Third, this reading of the book of Job identifies piety as a struggle, not a farce as a cyncial reading might insist. Although few would argue about the difficulty of achieving righteousness, in Job the very *definition* of piety (achieved righteousness) is called into question. Once again, no answers emerge dominant in this intellectual struggle. The God of Job does not bestow human value. Beauty and integrity must be fought for, captured from an unyielding universe. Job endeavors to wrest a sense of worth from God, and by extension, from his society as well.

Pitfalls of the Dissonantal Reading

The privileging of certain readings is unavoidable. The act of interpretation highlights certain textual features and inevitably suppresses others. Spivak (1976:lix) notes:

> The solution is not merely to say, "I shall not objectify." It is rather to recognize at once that there is no other language but that of "objectification" and that any distinction between "subjectification" and "objectification" is as provisional as the use of any set of hierarchized oppositions.

Derrida (1976:162) also deals with the problem of justifying one's methodology: "We must begin *wherever we are* and . . . it [is] impossible to justify a point of departure absolutely."

As a result, any act of interpretation does violence to a text: the text is transformed, enlarged, and reformed. Therefore, evaluative work is difficult but not impossible.

The text inexactly reflects societal conflicts. Winquist (1982: 36, 43) states, "Language was not a mirror of nature that established an identity. It was a reduplication of nature that established a difference . . . [The text] breaks with nature, draws away from nature, and establishes its own meaning." Literature is often "misread" as an exact reflection of societal dissonance. As a societal conflict passes into its textual form, two simultaneous transformations take place. First, the matter may pass from an oral to a written form (two kinds of verbal texts) and second, from a non-textual to a textual world. The process of entextualization does not necessarily clarify or obscure the conflict. It simply changes it. The text becomes the site for conflicting strategies of interpretation which often correspond to the various groups that engage in a power struggle in the non-textual world.

These conflicts are represented in the text as interpretive "lumps" that remain in the final textual product and are the most desirable sites of interpretation. What congeals in these lumps is the conflict that lay behind the production of the work. The written work then conjoins with the reader's context, creating a new reality. Subsequent to the point of fixity, the text is changed more through the generation of conflicting readings than overt textual manipulation. The text therefore reflects the concerns of various reading communities and not only the ancient concerns of the original tradents.

As a result, the "reflection" of the original nontextual world found in the text is never an exact picture. One therefore experiences difficulty in moving from the text to that indigenous world. There are not two "realms," the textual and non-textual. This dichotomy is a convenient fiction to simplify and describe the broad-ranging levels of experience. It would be just as easy to say that the world is in fact a text, and textual material exists as part of a world of artifacts.

Interpretations are overlaid on the reflected societal conflict. Not one interpretation, but a few contend for the text at most points throughout the history of its transmission. One cannot relegate even the simplest text to a single point of view. Often a single viewpoint is dominant, but in the more influential texts no clear strategy successfully suppresses the others.

Although the "archaeological" interest in its previous history remains relevant to a discussion of the text, it is by no means the only point at which a reader might enter Job. Rather, the various readings, the marriage of the ancient historical context and the milieu of the contemporary reader creates a new and unique interpretive moment. The forces that seek to shape a text are constrained by the permanent quality of letters on a page. Changes continue to take place, but are redirected primarily at the level of readings rather than in transformations of the text itself. The ancient conflicts therefore continue as recognizable features of the text.

Considerable distortion takes place when societal conflicts are codified into a text. The conflict will be deformed by the requirements of genre. The actual form of the material has a shaping function. What exist in a text therefore are not conflicts but rather conflicts *in narration*. Thus, to speak of a conflict without regarding its literary form is to bypass the text. The reader should not take recourse to generalities and abstractions, claiming that Job is *about* these philosophical or theological principles, such as "undeserved suffering" or "faithful obedience apart from expectation of reward." Even if the principles or formative structures are decontrusctive (absence, chaos or opacity), they are not the book of Job, but abstractions from Job.

Emerging Shapes in the Book of Job

The particular points of dissonance taken together begin to form shapes, patterns that arise from the reading.

The Shape of God

The text portrays non-textual reality as an absence, a formless cloud. Patterns emerge only indirectly. If declared normative or timeless, these patterns quickly dissolve back into the whole. The book of Job shapes deity in this manner. Various patterns form and dissolve as the book proceeds. God gambles irresponsibly, and damages his favored servant. Job seeks a defender (go'el) to defend him against God,[8] but God remains Job's only defender. God castigates those who defend this man; God praises and restores the one who questioned divine morality. God then restores Job and heals his pain.

This God inspires wonder and cynicism; he is both "buffoon" and final source of wisdom. He is everything (including those negative qualities usually denied to God) and nothing.

The shape of God becomes an absence due to the many conflicting and inconsistent pictures presented. Dissonance is produced by the moral resistance to the concept of radical monotheism in Israel, the absolute singularity of God (De Wilde 1981:29).[9]

A God who stands alone is responsible for *everything* that happens. Crenshaw observes, "A single deity kills and makes alive; bestows weal and woe" (Crenshaw 1987:376). Jung (1956:369) notes that "[Job] does not doubt the unity of God. He clearly sees that God is at odds with himself. As certain as he is of evil in Yahweh, he is equally certain of the good." This concept was challenged in both early and late periods in Israel by positing other supernatural beings who shoulder some of the blame. The book of Job bears traces of this theological tension.

In the settlement and early monarchic period, Canaanite polytheism offered an alternative; and in the time after Israel's exile, Persian dualism gained popularity. Neither alternative was fully satisfactory and what remained was a theological absence. There stood no alternative construal of God that offered adequate answers to the situations and problems that every Israelite was facing.

The dissonantal absence of any effective construal of God invites a present-day reconstrual of the god concept. Liberation might perhaps be achieved through a rejection of *any* concept of God, but I insist that one might utter statements concerning God that still give meaning in this present age. But if there is to be any twentieth century description of the shape of God in Job, it must acknowledge some divine responsibility for human evil, human stupidity and humanity's self-destructive tendencies. There remain no more effective theological subterfuges to maintain a defense against the reality of world-wide human pain and death, if indeed there ever were such.

One can remain hopeless, in an extended deconstructive moment, creating an ideology that imprisons and obscures the human identity. Or one can reconstrue the image of God on the principle of dissonance in the world.[10] God then would embody the impulse to dismantle inhuman societal assumptions, and also the impulse that generates dissatisfaction which results in change. I am by no means implying that change is some kind of ultimate value. Change often damages or destroys the good, and can be an instrument of oppression. The absence itself suggests some alternative constructions of deity.[11]

The beginning of a process of reconstructing the picture of God begins with two powerful articulations of absence. First is the absence of an effective and adequate language to describe God, and second, the absence of any reliable relationship of obligation between God and God's people.

In order to reconstruct God one must acknowledge the metaphorical nature of the construct,[12] and search for new construals of God that will allow a faithful trust relationship while including in the construal the presence of the experiences that previously pointed to divine enmity, God's moral failure.

In an as yet unpublished paper, "Metaphors of Faith," Lou Silberman discusses God's "unmetaphoricity." Going beyond the twin theological observations that the nature of God can only be communicated by metaphors and that there is no one metaphor adequate to describe God, Silberman claims that one may best describe God's very nature by the fact of God's unmetaphoricity, that the "metaphor of unmetaphoricity" is the most adequate descriptive framework to use when speaking of God.[13] "The only adequate metaphor [for God] is that which denies the possibility of metaphor" (Silberman 1985:35). God *is* the fact of his/her utter inscrutability. This is a dissonantal reading, but by no means the only one. Silberman (1985:35) claims for his construal:

> [This metaphor] forces us to examine and re-examine the metaphors—and they are, in great measure, dead metaphors. . . It reminds us of the vulnerability, the fragility of our metaphors that cannot bear the weight of dogma but shatter when taken out of the lively discourse in which they came to life.

James Crenshaw, in *Whirlpool of Torment* (1984), distinguishes two divine disasters that befall Job: divine absence (which may be identified with Silberman's concept of divine unmetaphoricity) and divine enmity, Crenshaw's focus. He writes (1984:64),

> In [Job] 13:25 Job likens himself to a helpless leaf that the wind drives hither and yon, or to chaff that has no control over its own destiny. The image of the creator of the entire universe chasing after a leaf or a tiny particle of chaff in order to crush it is poignant indeed.

This image of God as enemy is indeed another metaphor, but one that embraces the dissonantal features of Job. Certainly one may find God depicted as friend in the text of Job, but this is notably a minority (although by no means uninfluential) reading. As one looks at the shape of God in Job, one sees Silberman's dark cloud, but it often takes shape as a malevolent warrior, or, quoting Crenshaw (1977a:360),

> God deigned to reveal a face that inspired terror in one who had earlier dwelt in the shadow of his solicitous care, and

innocent sons and daughters fell victim to fatal blows wielded, with God's expressed permission, by a member of his heavenly court.

These two, in tension, both negative, deconstructive images, contend for the privilege of expressing the nature of God in Job.

The book of Job challenges the human community to reconstitute God by incorporating the characteristics that previous believing communities suppressed. The reader attempts to fill the absence at the heart of Job's picture with a less triumphalist view of God.[14] Humans have the authority to construe God in more inclusive fashions, truer to their experience. The fate of humanity depends on such a transformation; if the human race survives, it must change the way it thinks and the way it acts.[15]

The failure of the patriarchal, covenantal view of God to provide any effective answers to Job's suffering might suggest some alternative construals. Walter Brueggeman in his introduction to *Whirlpool of Torment* (1984:vii) notes, "The problem of the covenantal model is . . . that [it] becomes increasingly alienated from the realities of human pain, doubt, and negativity. Eventually the 'orthodoxy' of covenantal faith becomes repressive of human reality and censorious of those human experiences which are raw, nonconformist, and do not fit the grid of explanation." Many feminist theologians have suggested the need to describe God metaphorically in terms of the nurturing, fertile, world embracing characteristics, most commonly identified as "female,"[16] *the feminization of God.*

There has always been a minority position within the Hebrew Bible that affirmed manifestations of divine presence using female imagery (Lang 1975). In Job, absence (which itself suggests a womb-like space that births the world) offers the possibility of such a reconstrual of Israel's God.[17] It must be maintained that "female" modes of the divine historically have not been gentle, nurturing forces in society. One must note the contrary female image of the warrior goddess in Canaan. However, the reinstallation of these "feminine" qualities, one hopes, bodes well for a humanization and liberation of communal religion from oppressive, authoritarian structures.

Such a female construal of deity might suggest some tentative sources of comfort to Job's suffering. Whereas the older patriarchal conceptions of God can alleviate the suffering of Job, a nurturing deity (at least) hurts *with* Job and demonstrates a significantly greater degree of concern for Job's plight. (I have referred to Job's God using the masculine pronoun throughout, because the god of this text is presented in a decidedly patriarchal fashion.) Perhaps contemporary suffering would also be better served by such a way of speaking of God.

Also made possible by the dissonantal pictures of God is the *re-paganization of Yahwism*, by which is meant the reincorporation of the forces of the earth into the conception of Yahweh. The well-developed doctrine of Creation in ancient Israel commonly stopped short of identifying the powerful forces of creation with deity, although that identification is implicit in much of Israel's poetry.[18] Israel, in most of its literature, retained an anti-mythological bias. There are many sociological as well as theological reasons for this suppression, related to the bitter struggle between the Canaanite and the Israelite forces for domination of the land of Palestine. The mythological conceptions were nevertheless always there, underneath the surface, explicit during large periods of Israel's history, and widely spread through many segments of the population.

The dramatic ambiguity of divine construal in Job opens the way for the reintroduction of these ancient concepts, freeing humanity to cooperate and to create more interdependent relations in their religious activities.

This ambiguity also makes possible certain negative alternatives as well. We must admit that the triumphalist and authoritarian tendencies in late Israelite religion suppressed many harmful practices implied in the earlier syncretistic ideas.[19]

The Shape of Job

The book of Job never invalidates the reality of human pain. One can conceive of a reading that denied the importance and reality of Job's pain, but I have seen no such reading. There remains no effective refuge against human suffering, not even in the experience of mysterious divine presence. This intractability of human pain brings to attention the second shape that arises from the dissonantal text of Job: the figure of Job himself. These two ancient protagonists, God and Job, both loom large when reflecting on the book's dissonantal features. Job is a cry of pain, a terrifying scream that tears at the fabric of the universe. His personality is diffuse, but the impact of his pain convulses through every page of the book. Job not only embodies a physical suffering, his body ripped through by Yahweh's darts, but also a psychic torment marked by his abandonment by the human community and the absence of the longed for divine friendship. One necessarily feels the pain of Job. Also, one sees in the anguished face of Job the faces of many others in pain—the sick, the abandoned, the starving, the frightened. His pain widens the empathy of the reader to the scope of suffering common in the human community.

Job is human pride, the pride in achieving a certain level of righteousness; the pride in defending one's purity against both human and divine accusations, a Titanism that enables Job to challenge God.[20] The book of Job highlights the ability of a human to rebel against the constraints of religious interpretation and demand a new perspective that goes beyond a mere human passivity in the face of divine cruelty and arrogance.

Job embodies the human longing for divine presence. Job's scrupulous observance of the pious demands of his religion bespeaks his hunger for divine presence. He endures pain at his broken relationship with God, and shows his unwillingness to concede his argument, even when its legal basis (the law of retribution) had been shattered. His pleading for a divine intercessor and his lingering confidence that he would reappear before God, vindicated at some indistinct future date[21] demonstrate Job's persistent spiritual sensibilities.

Yet Job wavers. He gives up. But the divine longing returns. The quest for and belief in some sort of supernatural resolution to his problems is indomitable. As was demonstrated in chapter 3, the decisive resolution eludes him, but one senses that Job remains a questioning and seeking being, demanding divine presence.[22] At the core of his humanity, Job finds the instinct toward the divine cannot be conquered.

Job, in spite of his notably elitist attitudes towards his contemporaries,[23] becomes the archetypal human.[24] His situation is a proxy for every human situation, his strengths are the strengths of a human facing adversity. Job stands outside of his society, questioning its assumptions, injured by its insensitivity. A dissonantal reading of Job enables the reader to see contemporary political and theological assumptions through the lens of Job's sufferings, and to question the pious and superficial rationalizations given for human cruelty and oppression that keep people resting in an easy faith.

His formlessness, his vacillation between various positions, and his flitting between various emotional perches are also part of Job's shape. He is unrealized, fuzzy, and imprecise. His rash statements undercut his pious silence, and his irrational hope for vindication undermines his eloquent blasphemy. In spite of the assurances in the book's prologue that Job is an integrated human being, he is angst-ridden and tormented, with no precise center from which his personality flows. He reacts to his friends and his answers unfold in response to their accusations, not from any underlying ideological superstructure. Job's final responses to Yahweh's speeches, however interpreted, serve to underscore the ambiguity and difficulty of Job's position.

JOB AND THE HOLOCAUST

The book of Job demonstrates a strength that has resisted many attempts to suppress its radical dissonance. It breaks free of its own context and has the potential to speak powerfully to the modern situation. This contextual jump to the modern era does not directly add to a scholarly knowledge of Job, but apart from such a contemporary reflection upon the book by dealing with issues of value, Job will have only archival interest.

The dissonance in Job serves as a bridge to the modern world. As there are dissonantal access points that enable the interpreter to find essential qualities of Job, so too there are access points that lead one to the central sources of pain in the modern situation. Most prominent among these is the holocaust, the destruction of European Jewry by the Nazis. Some have noted the particular resonances between the plight of Job and the situation in Europe in the third and fourth decade of the twentieth century. This dialogue between an ancient work of literature and a modern disaster will serve to illustrate the manner in which such ancient documents may impinge upon a more contemporary situation.[25]

I noted earlier that the central fact of the person of Job, arising out of the contradictions in his character, is a cry of pain. As such, Job has served as an archetypal figure for all innocents isolated and in desperate agony. The senseless evil of the "final solution" immediately comes to mind as a prime example of innocent suffering carried to an unimaginable degree. The pain inflicted and experienced defies all human language enlisted to describe it.[26] It not only brings to mind the situation of Job but is bound to transform our reading of Job. Words such as "victim" and "innocence" are drained of meaning when brought to face this outrage.

Job walked toward an unimaginable silence when he sought God for answers adequate to face his situation. This impasse grows in proportion when an entire culture ransacks its religious traditions and returns bankrupt.[27] A few quotes from Elie Wiesel serve to illustrate this pain of abandonment.

> Never shall I forget that night . . . . Never shall I forget those flames which consumed my faith forever. Never shall I forget that nocturnal silence which deprived me, for all eternity, of the desire to live. Never shall I forget those moments which murdered my God and my soul and turned my dreams to dust. Never shall I forget these things, even if I am condemned to live as long as God himself. Never. (1960:44)
>
> [Weisel, on seeing a young child hanged, recalls,] Behind me, I heard the same man asking: "Where is God now?" And I heard a voice within me answer him: "Where is He? Here He is—HE is hanging here on this gallows . . . ." That night the soup tasted of corpses. (1960:76)
>
> [Again, on the possibility of fasting on Yom Kippur, he writes,] I did not fast, mainly to please my father, who had forbidden me to do so. But further, there was no longer any reason why I should fast. I no longer accepted God's silence. As I swallowed my bowl of soup, I saw in the gesture an act of rebel-

lion and protest against Him. And I nibbled my crust of bread.
In the depths of my heart, I felt a great void. (1960:80)

Suffering without respite coupled with a life drained of
meaning and goodness becomes unbearable. Joined to this (for
Job and the holocaust victims) is abandonment by the human
community as well. How must this refine and draw out the
remarkable nature of this torture! The possibility that some
representatives of human civilization might have sought in some
way to relieve such pain but instead refused, only makes the
pain and the abandonment worse.[28]

These parallels between Job and the victims of the concentration camps pay no heed to either the answers given to Job
by Yahweh or to Yahweh's restoration. Such palliatives in the
face of numbing affliction serve only to mock the sufferer and
make the dislocation more extreme. The dissonantal shape of
Job enables the reader to reject such easy answers to difficult
questions.

But what answers remain? The preceding discussion deconstructed the disfunctional models of God by exposing their
weaknesses and inner contradictions. The reconstructive suggestions that follow are necessarily modest. After listing some of the
elements that must necessarily be part of a new construal of
God, there remains the building of an entirely new myth. This
is beyond the scope of the present study.[29]

It is possible for these connections to give insight both into
the book of Job and into the situations of the holocaust. These
juxtaposed texts, Job and the holocaust, make strong demands
upon the human community:

1) The texts affirm the necessity of an awed silence in the
face of profound human suffering, with no attempt to justify it.

2) They affirm the necessity of violent protest against human
pain; not as an ordered indictment but rather an unrestrained
shriek, a howl of agony.[30]

3) They affirm the dignity of victims, the imperative not to
blame them, however oppression has dehumanized them. In the
face of such a betrayal of trust, the individual is both disorient-
ed and defiled. Such defilement must not be romanticized, but
we dare not ascribe blame in such a situation.

4) They affirm the bankruptcy of many older conceptions of deity that support the institutional sinfulness at the heart of much human suffering.

5) They affirm the necessity to reclaim human integrity which is not a given that the universe or deity generously provides, but rather something that must be grasped and held.

CONCLUSION

Elie Wiesel (1982:168-69), reflecting on the effect of the holocaust upon the intellectual and artistic life of Europe, stated:

> The sense of guilt played very little part in the determination of the European youth to build a new future out of the ruins around them. The arts—with the exception of painting—seemed to have hardly any interior connection with the terrible events which should have furnished their inspiration. No new philosophy was engendered, nor any new religion: the earth had trembled and men had stayed the same.

Suffering, even the most pointless and bewildering, enjoys some measure of redemption if people build upon the experience in the regeneration of their institutions and ideologies; if they *learn* from it. Wiesel laments that those who could best learn from the holocaust remained unchanged. World events following the Second World War have confirmed Wiesel's pronouncement.

Compounding the tragedy of Job, the destabilizing effect of Job's story had little effect on later developments in Israelite literature or institutions. Job created a crack in the door, a possibility for widening the response to misfortune and grief. But rather than reconstructing conceptions of deity to allow for ambiguity and absence, the Israelites labored to repair the traditional construals in the face of a new, disastrous situation.

One must not assume that the theological thinkers contrary to Job were sterile, lacking creativity. Rather, their rebuilding of the old ideas was characteristic of first-rate religious thinkers. Their contributions, however, diametrically opposed the dissonantal reading of Job, and this opposition merits attention.

First, in the midst of their sufferings, these reconstructive theologians ascribed responsibility for the disaster of the exile to the sins of the Israelite people.[31] With few exceptions, they did not malign deity, or question the retributional matrix in Israelite theological thought.

Then, faced with the breakdown of Israel's expectations concerning deity, the theologians of the exile and beyond resorted to greater and more specific determinations of God, rather than face the essential murkiness of any characterization of deity. They enlarged the scope of God's transcendent presence over Israel and the world, and developed a world-denying dualism to account for the presence of evil and suffering (Smith 1983:104). Stone (1983:86) speaks of an encroaching rigid piety in Israel developing subsequent to the fixing of the book of Job.

Rather than retain the openness to other nationalities present in the book of Job, post-exilic thought moved dramatically in the direction of an exclusivism that bordered on xenophobia. Job himself was not an Israelite. The book of Job builds on the literature and assumptions of many non-Israelite formulations. Exclusive religious practices such as circumcision and observance of the Sabbath were emphasized as important components of a righteous life; intermarriage and association with non-Israelites was strongly discouraged.

Finally, whereas Job affirms the importance and reality of present suffering as a vital determinant for theological constructions, exilic and post-exilic Israel became decidedly more future-oriented, looking to God to right the present wrongs and inequities in apocalyptic activity.[32] In acknowledging that God would rectify present injustice in some other world at some predetermined time, Israelite pain was driven inwards. The canonization of Job by this community, while allowing a measure of control by the interpreters as to what Job would say, speaks of the openness of this community to points of view different from its own. This is to their credit.

Apparently, the dissonantal voice of Job did not influence the interpretive communities that preserved its writing. When faced with the opportunity to destabilize religious perceptions in the mainstream of Israelite life, most of the religious leadership fled in terror. They banished the voice of skepticism in ancient Israel to the margin of Israelite thought.

Once again, and on a much wider scale, social and political forces have undermined the shared certainties of society, in this case all of Western civilization. Those who shape the dominant metaphors of society and those who submit to its shaping find themselves faced with an open-ended, unpredictable cosmos. Already, many have retreated into various forms of reaction and superficiality. McFague (1987:x) has observed concerning the contemporary situation.

> [that modern society faces] an apocalyptic sensibility, fueled in part by the awareness that we exist between two holocausts, the Jewish and the nuclear; and perhaps most significant, a growing appreciation of the thoroughgoing, radical interdependence of life.

Humans are challenged to tell new stories that embody this new reality, or tell old stories that have anticipated this society-wide *anomie*. The story of Job's wife embodies the qualities of the dissonantal reading that I have suggested and exemplifies a dissonantal response to the quality of terror that life offered.

She turns to her suffering husband and says to him, "You still keep your integrity! Blaspheme God and die!" The following reading of the story of Job's wife embodies the *meaning* of the entire book. Job's sufferings at the rejection of his spouse bespeaks all Job's losses, and the violence of Job's wife's vituperations against him personifies the manifold ways that the universe spat upon that unfortunate man. This narrative is a *metaphor* for the entire book of Job. The story of Job's wife becomes a parable that carries the prescriptive message of the entire work.

Many have tried to defend her reputation. They claim that she meant Job well and has just been misunderstood. The Septuagint and the Testament of Job expand on her role, trying to evoke more sympathy for this woman. She really had sacrificed and suffered for Job. She was sharing his pain and taking care of him.

The text will have none of this. She says, "curse God and die," an activity so dangerous that it is thought that this was a compassionate way to encourage Job to end his misery through suicide. But all are stunned by the callousness of her remarks. Perhaps she does Job a favor by encouraging him to strip away everything that kept him from seeing the pain that was always there. His wealth and complacency blinded him to spiritual reality.

Her words are so malicious and carefully chosen. She disparages his efforts at integrity, calling them pointless, having no effect. She tells him to blaspheme, the very thing he had always been so scrupulous to avoid. But she encourages him to tear apart and cast away the last vestiges of his pious rationalizations, the final barrier between him and the fearful void.

I suspect that most ancient Israelites shared knowledge of a terrible, public secret, one they would not dare to utter aloud: that outside of the ancient stories (and even in some of them—Jeremiah, Koheleth, Job and some Psalms, for instance) people were not struck dead when they cursed God. Not all were like the sons of Korah, or Nadab and Abihu, or Uzzah, or the children who mocked Elisha. There were certainly people in Israel who did curse God, and not just the unrighteous. Job could not face this fearful truth. Job's wife gave him courage to accuse the deity and *he does it well*. He curses God with an artistry and passion that is unsurpassed.

Job's wife made him aware of the issues that are at the heart of communal life: personal integrity and human discourse. On that ash heap he faced the precariousness of being human. When he was robbed of everything, he finally tasted the absence at the heart of things, and the utter fragility of all human knowledge. With her words, so brutal and cutting, she came close to personifying all of the abuse that Job received from the universe. If Job embodies the experience of human pain and abandonment, Job's wife represents the source of all human suffering. Eliphaz, Bildad, Zophar and even young Elihu argue with Job, annoying and angering him, but Job's pain was magnified and illuminated through the lens of *her* abuse. Job did blaspheme God; but he did not die. Ultimately, *that* is his integrity.

APPENDIX

NOTES

BIBLIOGRAPHY

INDEXES

APPENDIX

THE DATING OF JOB

Though lacking direct historical reference, attempts at dating the book of Job fallen into three different categories of inquiry: linguistics, literary dependence, and theological correspondence.

The language of the frame most closely resembles writing from an early period of Israelite literature (ninth to eighth century BCE), the same era that produced the Ancestral narratives. The center is a form of pre-Mishnaic late Hebrew, with many Aramaisms, as well as Persian and Egyptian loan words (Terrien 1954:887).

Clines (1985:127) describes the linguistic character of the frame "as plain as anything in the Hebrew Bible." Late writers, however, can (and have) used earlier patterns of speech. Linguistic dating cannot be a primary means of ascertaining the historical context, but can only supplement other methods. Indeed, the linguistic argument for early dating of the frame cuts both ways. Hurvitz (1974:18, 33, 34), while noting ancient influence in the frame narrative, identifies many characteristically late (post-exilic) elements of grammar and vocabulary (see also Day 1986:48). Kautsch (1900:22-23) deems vocabulary an unlikely source of reliable dating. Stylistic and linguistic considerations at most indicate that many features of the frame appear early, although there has been some significant late working of the material. Taken as a whole, however, the frame is unlikely to be of late origin.

Does Job's center quote other biblical books? If so the final form of the book of Job could not have been written before the other biblical books in question, and probably a good deal afterwards, when the book had achieved wide dissemination. Passages in Job's center resemble Jeremiah, Second Isaiah, and certain late Psalms.[1] It is notoriously difficult, however, to determine who is quoting whom.

Terrien (1954:888-889) has attempted to develop some objective criteria to determine the earlier work, and finds that Job (the center) quotes Jeremiah. He argues that Jeremiah's cursing of his birth and other confessional material is earlier because of its harshness and spontaneity, its colloquial abruptness. He sees the Joban parallels as more reflective, more refined, having a more polished style. Although his arguments are persuasive, one must at least concede the possibility that a skillful poet (as Jeremiah surely was) can adapt material, roughening the smooth edges of the work to make a theological point.

Terrien takes what appears to be a minority position in relationship to Second Isaiah, claiming that this exilic poet is reflecting on the poet in Job, and not the other way around (889). Van Selm (1985:6) and others, however, assume Isaianic priority. The identification of the passages in question as quotations is not simple. In this case, too, Job resists attempts to date its parts decisively. It is impossible to determine, except in the most speculative ways, which work came first, or to determine literary dependency at all. Perhaps both texts draw on earlier and now lost textual material or cultural concepts. The controversial nature of literary adjudications should make a careful reader suspicious of the ultimate reliability of this method of dating.

Dating based on theology has become the most common means of pinpointing Job's historical context. But theology does not develop in a linear fashion, going consistently from the less to the more complex, attaining greater sophistication with the passage of time. The reality is far more complicated. Van Selm (1985:7) has asserted, "History knows of no such linear, and generally valid, development in concepts and ideas. In every age there are dissidents . . . [Job] continually protests the prevailing opinions of contemporaries, opinions that cannot be dated either, but rather tend to speak for all ages."[2]

Two factors must be identified to establish theological dating. A theological position must be isolated as the distinct property of a particular era, and a clear expression of that theological position in a certain portion of Job must be ascertained. Attempts have been made to do this with both Job's frame and center.

Various aspects of the frame's theology have been identified as characteristically early. They include a view of retribution that, it is argued, would have more likely pertained before the Israelite experience of exile. Job's piety and his prosperity in the prologue, and the certain and abundant restoration of Job's family and property in the epilogue, reflect a period when Israel's fortunes were relatively prosperous.[3] The importance of sacrifice in the frame reflects a time when such cultic practices were widely accessible to the population, when most Israelites accepted the effectiveness of a decentralized sacrificial cultus. Much later Israelite literature attacked current notions of the efficacy of sacrifice (the prophets) or declared such activity meaningful only when performed by the approved priestly hierarchy (Kinet 1983: 30). Sacrifice finds no significant place in the center of Job.

The Edomite (non-Israelite) nationality of the main character does not commonly function as a positive role model to the Israelites after the exile, the height of Jewish xenophobia (Terrien 1954:888).[4] But the post-exilic books of Ruth and Jonah, notably sympathetic to the non-Israelite, make this an unreliable means of dating the book of Job early or late.

The presence of the Satan figure has been used to prove both an early and a late date for the frame of Job. Its presence has been described both as an ancient mythological motif and a later theological concept imported from Persia in the sixth century. There are three different ways that the evidence has been treated.

First, many have seen the Satan as discharging a role in the ancient Canaanite pantheon. Haag has described the heavenly court as "demoted" Canaanite deities.[5] Kluger notes that the equality of God and the Satan represents an older polytheistic conception that was only transformed to conform with exclusivistic Yahwistic ideas (1967:95, 98).

Terrien argues that without the Satan, the story would make no sense, it being essential that Job's innocence be established without question. He also notes "The motif of a wager between Yahweh and a member of the divine assembly has a popular, picturesque, even humorous flavor which suggests a polytheistic background. . . and is quite incompatible with the monotheistic spirit and the reverent tone of biblical editors generally" (1954:884; see also Gordis 1965:69).

Others have allowed that the heavenly council may be dated early, but ascribe the Satan figure to a later tradent interpolated by the poet. Kluger (1967) sees the Satan as a highly developed and late concept in Israelite theological conception. Kinet also acknowledges a late dating, the inclusion of Satan (he says) intended to exculpate Yahweh from the responsibility for Job's affliction (1983:31). Hurvitz notes reference to the Adversary as a specific personage in the court of heaven as exclusively late (1974:19).[6] Weiss presents three different meanings for the term *satan* in the Hebrew Bible: 1) a term describing a certain type of behavior, one who opposes; 2) the title of an officer in the employ of God, a prosecutor, prefixed with the definite article; and 3) the proper name of a celestial being whose role is to incite humanity against God. Job, according to Weiss, employs the second usage, along with Zechariah. He therefore would characterize this usage as early postexilic, certainly not from the monarchical period (Weiss 1983:35-36; see also Lévêque 1981:207).

Finally, the entire heavenly court has been described as a late motif employed by the poet.[7] In such a case, tradents would have added the divine assembly to the frame at a late stage in its development, thus putting God in a more favorable light. In earlier stages of the text Yahweh had borne full responsibility for the affliction of Job (Kinet 1983:31).[8]

Regarding the theological dating of the center, its rebellious and skeptical note is thought to characterize a profoundly (theologically) disillusioned people (Duquoc 1983:82).[9] Tsevat (1966:101) has noted:

> Yet for all the difficulty of dating, the overwhelming majority
> of scholars, for a variety of reasons, date the book of Job
> between the sixth and the fourth centuries B.C. Now that is
> the very period in which the earlier doctrine of collective
> retribution . . . had lost its sway without yet being replaced by

the doctrine of individual retribution in the world-to-come . . . Thus it would seem clear that the sixth through the third centuries represented that one period in the history of biblical religion which is not covered, or, at best, very scantily covered, by one or the other form of this idea of divine justice. It is in this period that the problem of the suffering of the innocent is most likely to have been answered in a way other than, hence opposed to, that of divine justice=retribution. And this is the very period to which the book of Job is commonly dated.

Israel had been taken captive and its cultic and political life was destroyed by foreign invaders. These events correspond most closely to the theological picture in the center of Job.

This form of theological dating creates significant problems, however. Individuals often hold philosophical positions that do not correspond to corporate or community crises. The world of ideas conjoins with history in a complex fashion and is not easily analyzed by recourse to a one-on-one identification.

Precise dating of the frame is impossible because, in giving the frame a more "modern" tinge, the author of the center tampered with it to some degree. It is difficult to determine reliably which parts of the frame predate the center, and which parts were added later, whether by the final tradent or by one of the intermediary figures. For instance, there has been controversy about the originality of the wife, the Satan, and the entire heavenly assembly, among those who see the folk tale as the ancient precursor of the book of Job.

Evidence for the Legendary Job

External evidence points persuasively to the existence of a folk story that predates and underlies the development of canonical Job. Other similar folk stories exist in cognate cultural settings.[10] Nahum Sarna has noted that the frame of Job displays many of the characteristics of epic forms that existed in other cultures in the ancient Near East. These features include a mythological flavor, and stylized poetic patterns (1957:17-18).[11]

Additionally are various references to Job in sources external to the book that would seem to refer to a story developing in a different direction than the canonical Job. Ezekiel (14:12-20) refers to Job, saying:

> The word of the LORD came to me: O mortal, if a land were to sin against Me and commit a trespass, and I stretched out My hand against it and broke its staff of bread, and sent famine against it and cut off man and beast from it, even if these

three men—Noah, Daniel, and Job—should be in it, they
would by their own righteousness save only themselves—
declares the LORD God . . . those three men in it would save
neither sons nor daughters; they alone would be saved, but
the land would become a desolation.

Many have noted how this account diverges from the canonical
Job. There is, for instance, no trace of rebelliousness or the questioning of God in Ezekiel's account of the "righteous Job,"[12] and even
more striking is Job's inability to intercede for anyone but himself.
Job's prayer in Ezekiel's account is not effective for his children, but is
effective for himself (Van Selm 1985:6; Gordis 1965:69). In the
prologue of canonical Job, the patriarch offers prayer for his children.
In the epilogue, Job prays for his friends with great success. In the
center, Job can hardly manage to pray for himself, and his prayer
reaches an astoundingly non-responsive God. It is therefore widely
assumed that the story to which Ezekiel referred was not canonical
Job, but rather "an epic of Job well known to his contemporaries."
Weiss (1983:16) notes, "Ezekiel would never have made mention of
Job if he had only known our story of Job. There probably circulated
many legends about the righteous Job which told of the hero's lot in
many and varied ways."

It must be conceded however that this assumption is speculative.
One must allow for the possibility that people reading canonical Job
would selectively ignore key passages to gain a certain theological
impression, due to the dominant philosophical environment in which
interpretation is made. The references are so divergent however that
a more radical breach between the two readings seems justified. The
assumption that Ezekiel had access to a different story is therefore still
likely. The book also points to the circulation of a tale not correspondent to canonical Job.

The book of James (5:11) refers to "the steadfastness of Job."
Bloch (1972:116) says, "The most bitter of men has been made out to
be the most patient . . . The words from the opening, 'The Lord gave
and the Lord has taken away,' have together with those from the
ending, 'The Lord blessed the latter days of Job more than his beginning,' succeeded in extinguishing the fiery center of the book."
Patience is in fact the one virtue that seems farthest from the Job
depicted in the Israelite story (MacDonald 1898:139).[13]

It is presumed here, therefore, that the frame is an adaption of the
earlier folk story with few changes, notably the addition of the center,
an extensive debate between Job and his friends, and the appearance
of Yahweh preceding the legendary resolution. Clearly, the poet
thought the folk story important enough to retain (with some alter-
ations) yet was in need of his or her contribution as well.

NOTES

NOTES TO CHAPTER 1
THE DISPARATE TEXT

1. Althusser's definition of ideology is "the imaginary representation of the subject's relationship to his or her real conditions of existence" (Jameson 1981:181). Macherey identifies ideology as "The operation of a fictional system [which] ultimately produces an ideological effect" (1978:296). In distinction from "theory," [both theory and ideology are mental constructs but] "ideology claims to correspond to reality" (Jameson 1972:104). Terry Eagleton defines it as "the largely concealed structure of values which informs and underlies our factual statements . . . the ways in which what we say and believe connects with the power-structure and power relations of the society we live in" (1983:114). Michel Foucault objects to the use of the term "ideology" because "it always stands in virtual opposition to something else which is supposed to count as truth" (1984:60).

2. Stephen Zelnick notes that "In traditional Marxist criticism, ideology is considered a false knowledge, opposed to some truth that is easily ascertained. For Macherey, as for Althusser, ideology *cannot be eluded*, [emphasis added] for no one lives science. Indeed, ideology is understood as an historical force alongside material forces" (1979: 213).

3. Robert Scholes defines metacommentary as "a procedure which seeks to locate and expose for any given text, the 'interpretive master-code,' already in place as an interpretive method or approach" (1984:270-271).

4. My view of gaps must be distinguished from that of Meir Sternberg (1987:186-229). The following are significant differences. For Sternberg:

1) Gaps are part of a generally harmonizing impulse, which is never questioned. Gaps function as an absence to be filled (188, 191, 198, 201).

2) Gaps are intrinsic to the text, thrust upon the reader in an objective fashion. They are not the cooperative product of a reading event (189).

3) He emphasizes (perhaps due to his choice of texts) gaps as a lack of details, rather than as a clash of details and ideologies, sometimes a surplus of meanings (193).

4) He pays scant interest to the ideological implication of gaps because he has declared that the literary approach (a term he disparages) (3) attends primarily to aesthetic considerations (193).

5) He accepts the Aristotelian notion of non-contradiction in real life and thus creates a radical disjunction between text and "real life" (228).

In contrast, I must observe that gaps do not always cooperate with some writer's "intention," but often activily resist any larger aesthetic or ideological program. All texts are not products of "conscious artristry."

5. Although these books by Jameson and Macherey make separate contributions, they present a significantly unified approach to literature. They disagree on many particulars (noted where relevant) but their analysis of dissonance is substantially similar. The Post-Modernists have been most closely identified with this kind of meta-commentary. Jameson and Macherey maintain that interpretation is still possible and so prove more useful in an interpretation of Job.

6. Spivak defines Structuralism as "an attempt to isolate the general structures of human activity . . . A structure is a unit composed of a few elements that are invariably found in the same relationship within the 'activity' being described . . . The structure is defined not so much by the substantive nature of the elements as by their relationship" (1976:lv). She quotes Lévi-Strauss who describes Structuralism as:

1) The study of unconscious linguistic structures.

2) The study of these structures in terms of their relationships.

3) The study of the system or systems behind the linguistic phenomenon (lvi).

7. In the United States, excepting from those who gravitated to Structuralism, there was a movement known as New Criticism, which in fact predated Russian Formalism. This Southern School of literary analysis abandoned the popular historical approach to writing and elucidating literature, embracing instead a radical textual autonomy, apprehended through a mystical merger of reader with the text, whereby the text unveils its message. Although producing marvelous readings of influential poems, this movement could not sustain its sense of a shared human aesthetic when faced with the unfettered pluralism dominant in the latter half of the twentieth century. Blackmur (1971) provides an effective introduction to New Criticism. See Jameson (1971) and Lentricchia (1980) for meaningful criticisms of the movement.

8. Jameson notes a particular resonance between the structure and the historical considerations of the text. Whereas the content would tend to conceal the historical-rootedness of a text, the structure reveals the hidden dynamics that formed the written material (1981: 280).

9. For Saussure, objects such as nouns and verbs do not exist, but only the relations. The individual "units" are only imaginative constructs. One sign is seen as it is only in terms of its difference from other signs (Jameson 1972:17).

10. There is some discussion of gaps or absences in most modern critical approaches. Although differing in where they locate these disjunctions, the parallels are significant. Jameson, in a discussion of Formalism observes, "No text has an ultimate meaning but each text is necessarily interpreted because of an ontological lack within itself, and each interpretation in turn becomes a new signifier that must be interpreted, in infinite regression" (1972:177). Macherey states: "The work exists above all by its determinate absences, by what it does not say, in its relation to what it is not . . . this meaning . . . is not in the work but by its side, on its margins, at that limit where it ceases to be what it claims to be" (1978:154). There is always a conflict of meaning, and "the conflict is not a sign of an imperfection; it reveals the inscription of an otherness in the work, through which it maintains a relationship with that which it is not, that which happens at its margins . . . In both the empirical and idealist theories there is a suppression of literature's most revealing feature—its discontinuity, diversity, disparity, and multivocality. The ideologically repressed returns in the eruptions of these discontinuities" (Zelnick 1979:214).

11. See also the Russian Formalist concept of *ostranenie* (defamiliarization), in which the project of producing a renewal of perception is seen as determining the very structure of the individual literary work (Jameson 1972:75-79, Ferguson 1974:312). These silences participate in dissonance. Although in Structuralism, "difference" appears to be static, an eternal opposition rather than a dynamic struggle, this concept constitutes an important step towards understanding the disharmony that exists within a text, which is, in fact, quite unstable (Seller 1972:294).

12. Macherey quotes Lévi-Strauss: "We ascertain what the myth has to say by constituting its 'structure.' . . . In reality, the structure is the very space of difference" (1978:153). He notes that societies utilize myth to resolve unspoken conflicts on the psychic and spiritual realm (Jameson 1972:197).

13. Jameson faults Structuralism for its inability to account for change, events in time. It can therefore never reach from the signified (the text) to the signifier (non-textual reality) (1972:59). Sternberg (1987:xii) says "Form has no value or meaning apart from communicative (historical, ideological, aesthetic) function." Robert Weimann (1969:92) observes that "Literature is not an object to be contemplated, but a process in time." Jameson (1971:392) notes that the literary product is fully involved at every stage in the social and economic world in which it exists.

NOTES TO CHAPTER 1

14. As a result, Structuralism seeks to avoid dealing with wider issues, staying close to particular texts [according to Jameson] (1972: 209). Jameson (1972:89) seeks to "historicize" Structuralism by noting that "literary works . . . speak a language of reference . . . [they] emit a kind of latent message about their own process of formation . . . the work is solidified, the product of the end result of production."

15. Funt (1973:413) observes that Structuralists are "the modern mystics of reason, presenting us with the concrete results of their own meditations as images of the process of thought—objects for our meditation. What we are presented with ultimately are complex and very elegant hieroglyphical representations of the mystery, as Jameson puts it, of the incarnation of meaning in language." Jameson (1972: 194) criticizes Structuralism for having claimed a new type of objective science: semiology. Spivak (1976:lvii) defines a structure as "the natural object *plus* the subjective intelligence of the structuralist" [emphasis added]. See also Foucault 1984:103.

16. "Vulgar" Marxism would see only Socialist Realism as "good" contemporary art and would denigrate any specimen of creativity that did not adequately share the particular view of Marx's idealized society. See Macherey's discussion of early Marxist criticism of Jules Verne (1978:237).

17. For instance, Lucian Goldman would look for homologies, parallel structures in literature and public life (economics). Jameson does not see this as helpful (1972:212).

18. For Jameson, history is the only absolute in a system that denies the existence of absolutes. It is "the ultimate ground as well as the untranscendable limit of our understanding" (Jameson 1981:100). It is not a text; it has no boundaries and is therefore "infinitely totaliz-able" (53), and therefore "subsumes other interpretive modes and systems" (47). For Macherey, history is not such a transcendent force, but is the widest horizon, the arena of ideological conflict.

19. Jameson disagrees that the production of literature can be compared so easily to the production of material commodities. Neither Jameson nor Macherey though, deny that there are important similarities among the modes of production.

20. "For Macherey, literature is never what it appears to be. Instead, a literary work must be reconstructed according to its ideological determinations" (Zelnick 1979:213).

21. Jameson has built upon this structuralist insight. As John D. Erickson notes, Jameson sees other codes of interpretation—ethical, psychoanalytic, myth-critical, semiotic, structural, and theological—as limited by their "strategies of containment" (Erickson 1983:627). For Jameson, pure Marxism has no strategy of containment although he concedes that existent systems of Marxism do indeed engage in ideological struggle.

22. More extreme statements would boldly state that nothing exists except the textual world.

23. The third movement of Marxist Criticism, represented by Jameson and Macherey, a kind of "reconstruction" of the text, will be treated at the end of the chapter.

24. Frances C. Ferguson observes Jameson's dependence upon Derrida's "recent questioning of the privileged position of the very structures of Structuralism" (1974:313).

25. Spivak (1986:xiii) notes that while the absence is a source of unhappiness to the structuralists, for the Post-Modernist it is "the joyous affirmation of the play of the world and the innocence of becoming, the affirmation of a world of signs without fault, without truth, without origin, offered to an active interpretation." She goes on to say, "Derrida seems to show no nostalgia for a lost presence" (xvi).

26. Scharlemann (1982:81) defines deconstruction: "to analyze the elements of the structure of thought and trace them back to their beginning . . . in order to discover the experience that is at the basis of the structure."

27. "Derrida proffers the unlimited 'play' of signification itself, open at both ends; at no point in the sign process can we say that the 'meaning' of a sentence and text has been secured" (Raschke 1982:7).

28. Jameson attacks the Deconstructionist claim that writing is all there is, as in fact a claim to an ultimate horizon. If so, it is a horizon whose hermeneutical function is minimal.

29. Macherey observes, "The ideological plan is inevitably reversed by its execution, because an ideology cannot function as a particular text. By particularizing the ideology, it is inevitably deconstructed" (1978:218).

30. Raschke (1982:13) states, "Thus both philosophy and theology, through an inquiry into the forms of writing and their semantic peculiarities, can uncover their own agenda and aim."

31. Spivak (1986:lxxvii) says, "The fall into the abyss of deconstruction inspires us with as much pleasure as fear. We are intoxicated with the prospect of never hitting bottom."

32. "The omega moment of deconstruction is when the movement of deconstruction deconstructs itself" (Raschke, 1982:31). For Derrida (Spivak 1986:xviii) deconstruction is "the strategy of using the only available language while not subscribing to its premises, operating according to the vocabulary of the very thing she delimits."

33. These points of dissonance will not be equally important in each examined text. Some will be more prominent than others either because of the characteristic features of that particular text, or in the case of ancient literature, because the effects of time have hidden much of the crucial information.

34. Many will take exception to the use of the word "inevitable," asserting that there are harmonious texts and texts in conflict with

society. It is my position that all texts, regardless of the originally intended function, generate significant conflict in their own society, as well as in subsequent reading and editing contexts. Literature (as opposed to oral speech) exposes and breaks down ideology.

35. Macherey (1978:48) writes: "The author certainly makes decisions, but, as we know, his decisions are determined; it would be astonishing if the hero were to vanish after the first few pages, unless by way of parody. To a great extent the author also encounters the solutions and resigns himself to handing them on. His narrative is discovered rather than invented, not because he begins at the end, but because certain directions are firmly closed to him. We might say that the author is the first reader of his own work . . . it is the reading of a previously established model."

Foucault (1984:118-119) states, "The author is not an indefinite source of significations which fill a work; the author does not precede the works; he is a certain functional principle . . . by which one marks the manner in which we fear the proliferation of meaning." "The author also serves to neutralize the contradiction that may emerge in a series of texts" (1984:111).

36. Macherey (1978:133) observes that by the very nature of its reduction to writing, ideology is "broken." The effect of literature exposes ideology. "Ideology is . . . turned inside out . . . [literature's] function is to present ideology in a non-ideological form . . . The work has an ideological content, but . . . it endows this content with specific form . . . literature challenges ideology by using it." See also 191. Elsewhere he notes that "[the work] is also influenced by the formal function of the writer and by the problems of his individual existence" (p. 53). Mark C. Taylor (1969:71) quotes Altizer: "Through inscription, presence becomes absence, and becomes actual as absence, and that absence is the self-enactment of presence." Writing reifies the life-giving symbols, killing them.

37. Spivak (1986:lxxv) "We shall see the text coming undone as a structure of concealment, revealing its self-transgression, its undecidability."

38. The work is produced with readers in mind. "The conditions that determine the production of the book also determine the forms of its communication" (Macherey 1978:69-70). "The writer is called upon . . . to resolve . . .the determinate question, 'What must I do to be read?'. . . The act of writing is not simply determined by an individual decision" (ibid:72). Sartre sees the role of the public as forming, to a large extent, what writers write. The writer limits his or her audience by what he or she chooses to explain at length and what is assumed to be known by the audience. Some groups are thereby privileged, and others are left out (Jameson 1972:28).

39. Occasionally rival distribution networks function underground. They exist in complex interrelationships with the more established

chains of distribution, but they still serve to put writing into the hands of those who want to read it and they too exert influence upon the act of writing.

40. Foucault notes: "To comment is to admit by definition an excess of the signified over the signifier . . . there is always a certain amount of signified remaining that must be allowed to speak" (Macherey 1978:148). This excess is often given explicit form in these explanatory writings. Rick D. Moore has explored a transitional section between Job 1, 2 and the contrasting text of chapter 3 (1983:17-31).

41. See Jameson (1981:29) for a discussion of reading as allegorization. This might also be known as "transcoding," a translation from one code to another.

42. Historical explanations for these conflicts do not fully interpret a text. Rather they provide a useful key to some of the sources for texts. See Sternberg (1987:41) who distinguishes "ideological, historiographic and aesthetic" elements that might concern an interpreter.

43. "And is not the text the stage or the field upon which the struggle of interpretation is enacted or played?" (Taylor 196:63). Philip Wheelwright (1962:72) speaks of a literary phenomenon similar to dissonance: "diaphor." He contrasts two types of metaphor: epiphor "applies [a] word to something else on the basis of, and in order to indicate a comparison with what is familiar," and diaphor, "where two dissimilar ideas are juxtaposed, thus producing new meanings" (78). See also Frank Burch Brown (1982:45): "Unlike epiphor, diaphor creates new meanings through . . . the sheer juxtapositioning of seemingly unlike, heterogeneous semantic elements, the referents of which are linked less by similarity or rational connection, than by sheer contiguity and intuitive affinity."

44. This seems to be Macherey's position as to the explanation of dissonance. He states (1978:117): "It is precisely because the doctrine is inadequate to the data, that the structure of the work is contradictory. Once it has been stripped of all the elements borrowed from ideology, might not the intrinsic function of literature be to furnish perceptions distinct from the doctrine, perceptions upon which an authentic knowledge might be grounded?"

NOTES TO CHAPTER 2:
COMPOSITION AND DISSONANCE

1. Moshe Greenberg (1987:283) observes, "The chief literary . . . problem of Job is its coherence."

2. Piety is not a Joban word, unless it is identified with the term *fear* in the prologue and chapter 5. The concept, however, is operative in the book of Job. It might be defined as 1) the respect for taboos concerning blasphemy, 2) the support of societal/theological con-

straints, 3) behavior consistent with one's concept of deity and 4) behavior that warrants social approval.

3. Many commentaries discuss this. Moore's contrast (1983:22, 26) between Job's resignation to his fate in 1:21 and Job cursing the day of his birth in chapter 3 is most instructive and compelling. He posits a deliberate attempt on the part of the poet to criticize and ridicule the Job depicted in the frame. See discussion in Vermeylan 1986:31-33.

4. Meir Weiss' book (1983) is the only full length treatment of the frame (in this case, only the prologue) that I have been able to find in the modern era. Earlier, I might note Karl Kautzsch 1900.

5. Bruce Vawter (1983:43-44) quotes John L. McKenzie: "Had it not been for the Israelite poet, that sickly story would no doubt have sunk into deserved oblivion."

6. See Driver (1921:xxvi, xxxv), Terrien (1954:884-885), Moore (198:17) and Rowley (1970:9-10) for complete summaries of the scholars who defend the various views.

7. Habel (1985:84) notes, "The language of the book reflects a literary unity which embraces an inner tension reflecting divergent perspectives on the same reality." "Might it [the frame] not have been a created framework to hold together the speeches?" (25). Habel (51) and other literary critics develop a false argument against the apparent radical disjunction of the frame and the center. No one of whom I am aware has ever made such a radical assertion. In reference to the literary connections between the frame and the center, Terrien (1954: 88) observes "The linguistic affinities between the narrative and the poem probably suggest that the poet was intimately acquainted with the prose story and has erected his poetic monument upon its foundation." Yair Hoffman (1981:60-170) argues from certain literary resonances that aspects of the frame make no sense apart from the dialogues. He argues from this, unconvincingly I believe,for the literary dependence of the frame upon the dialogues.

8. Van Selm (1985:7) notes references to the center [dialogue] in the epilogue, and also points to the highly sophisticated and artistic nature of the frame, and argues for unitary authors: Vermeylan (1986:5) discusses the idea of unitary authorship, giving it a psychological explanation. This is contained in a survey of the various possible positions.

9. For instance, Robert M. Polzin's (1977:107) driving assumption is that the book does make sense because it has affected many people deeply. Habel (1985:24) insists on interpreting verses in their context, which assumes that they have a context, that is, a positive, logical one—one that affirms the existence of a whole. These assumptions are by no means self-evident.

10. The question as to exactly how much freedom the poet had in fashioning the original folk story will be dealt with below. See also

Georg Fohrer (1983:24). Note that William Barron Stevenson (1947: 21-22) stands almost alone in the contention that the poem was meant originally to be read by itself.

11. Rolf Knierim (1973:448) notes concerning this methodological problem, "After a genre has been identified with great effort on morphological grounds, those studies continue to look for a setting at any cost, postulating, creating, fabricating one even if—sometimes admittedly—there is no evidence for it."

12. Claus Westermann (1983:17-18) states that by establishing an historical explanation of the dissonance in Job, one has merely postponed the solution. Most assume that the historical solution ends the matter, but it is only the beginning.

13. Terrien (1954:890) claims a historical reference to the deportations in Job 12:17-19, which is in fact a common poem of reversal, the powerful becoming weak and the weak strong; and a reference to moon worship in Job 31:26-28 which he relates to Jeremiah 44:15-19. There is, however, no linguistic similarity between the passages, moon worship being common in all ages. This demonstrates how hard people have searched for some bare historical reference, and how futile this search has been. Albert Cook (1968:xi) points out that the book of Job was repeatedly shifted in the order of canonicity, thus indicating the tentative historical understanding of this book.

14. Habel (1985:42) for instance, sees dating as ultimately insignificant because the book has a universal appeal and quality and a picture of God which would be uncomfortable in any era. Roberts (1977:109) in a more mature, hard-hitting analysis notes correctly that "Job simply ignores Israel's epic and prophetic traditions." He avoids the important significance of this observation when he states: "The actual date of the composition of Job is largely irrelevant (113). See also Van Selm 1985:7.

15. See the Appendix for a more detailed discussion of the traditional methods of dating the book of Job.

16. I do not mean to imply that a lack of scholarly consensus in itself is sufficient ground to reject a method. In the case of Job, however, I see this lack of consensus as indicative of a particular literary feature that is significant for the analysis of the book, its resistance of historicizing. This resistance is a dissonantal feature.

17. The interpreter must be wary of any claim that the post-exilic period was devoid of creativity, life and religious vibrancy. Developments in cult and law are unsurpassed during this period (Ackroyd, 1968:5-12). I contend however, that the theologians of this period revised their traditions to meet their own needs (as do all cultures) and their needs were narrowly defined in terms of the generation of support for Israel's religious institutions.

18. James G. Williams (1971:238-39) refers to Israel's "collapse of world view," and makes reference to Tillich's phrase "a land of broken symbols."

19. Knierim (1973:437) defines *Sage* (folk narrative) as requiring "three constituents (one or more motifs), a fixed form, and above all—a content of belief. [This rubric] has also been supplemented by the category of social function." On such a basis, I identify this *ur*-form of Job as legendary folk material.

20. This story was not original with the Israelite sages, but rather was lifted (probably through some intermediaries) from other cultures that had a class that considered intellectually the terrors of their age and how to cope with them. It was in fact a vast effort to impose order upon the universe, to capture some consistency from randomness. Attempts were also being made to impose order mythologically (Ancestors, Creation, Mosaic narrative), in a legal way (Torah) or an emotive way (the prophets).

21. Examples of other ancient Near Eastern Job-like stories are "A Dispute Over Suicide" (Pritchard 1969:405-406) and "The Protests of the Eloquent Peasant" (407-410)—both Egyptian—and "I Will Praise the Lord of Wisdom" (434-437) and "A Pessimistic Dialogue Between Master and Servant" (437-438)—both Babylonian.

22. Kautsch (1900:18) suggests considerable differences between the frame of canonical Job and the original legendary material. While not claiming a complete correspondence between the two, I contend a substantial continuity.

23. Pope (1973:xxvi) asserts: "How much of the ancient folk tale is preserved by the Prologue-Epilogue, and what modifications the author of the poetic Dialogue had to make in the old story is impossible, at this time, to determine. Probably very little of the old tale has been lost because the Prologue and Epilogue together present a fairly complete story."

24. Westermann (1981:17) points to the ancestral style of the narrative. Whedbee (1977:5) notes the fairy tale beginning, the vaguely defined land, the stylized numbers, the repetition and stylized characterization. Sarna (1957:14-15) notes the "epic substratum for the folk story."

25. See Appendix for a fuller discussion of the external evidence for the existence of an ur-form for legendary Job.

26. Snaith (1968:6, 8) denies the presence of the friends in the original story. Vawter (1983:37) views the friends as the original tempters in the folk story. Robertson (1977:53) feels that originally the speeches of the friends argued that God was unjust.

27. Vawter (1983:35) suggests that "Job's wife is a new invention introduced into the story to assume the role of tempter formerly fulfilled by Job's friends—who now quite obviously have been accorded an entirely different function in the poetry." Crenshaw (1987:382)

contends that "the oldest form of the story lacked this character [the Satan] and viewed Job's wife as the antagonist."

28. Kember Fullerton (1924:117) stands almost alone in noting the irony of the prologue.

29. Crenshaw (1980:5-6) demonstrates that skepticism arose early in Israel's history.

30. My difficulties here exemplify the struggle to historicize an anti-historical book. If Satan were a late addition the picture of the folk story (although not the present form of the story) would be transformed.

31. The Hebrew word here used, sût is softened considerably in the Septuagint. It changes to legô (propose or speak). See Henry S. Gehman (1949:231).

32. Day (1986:62) contends that the absurdity of the restoration is a function of the folk genre and is therefore defensible from an aesthetic and theological viewpoint. However, the patent offense necessarily remains. Duncan R. MacDonald (1895:65) argues [concerning the restoration of Job's family] "We can only explain this as an instance of oriental apathy . . . Yet there is no apathy in Job's own words when he looks back upon the time 'when Shaddai was yet with me, when my sons were around me.' (19:5) The grief of the man who said that was not to be appeased by a new family growing up around him." Williams (1971:250) notes, "The poet does not take the epilogue to the book of Job seriously, except insofar as it enhances the irony of the dialogue and theophany."

33. Moore (1983:20) notes, "The prose story rather emphasizes that God, for reasons unknown to humankind, may cause evil to fall upon the good." Although Moore minimizes Job's restoration, his return to wealth and his renewed reputation and family keep the issue of a predictable god an open question.

34. Janzen (1985:17-18) quotes Booth's definition of irony: "Most simply put, the recognition of irony in a text is the recognition that . . . some statements cannot be understood without rejecting what they seem to say . . . which undercuts their apparent meaning." Clines (1985:127, 134) identifies the character of the frame as "false naivety," and skillfully demonstrates the layers of complexity underneath the seemingly simple surface.

35. A. De Wilde (1981:37) feels that overemphasis on the picture of Job presented by the frame has diminished Job's usefulness. The frame cannot, however, be dismissed so lightly. Gordis (1965:71) states, "The prose narrative which has reached us is no naive, unsophisticated story. It bears all the characteristics of literary craftsmanship of the first order."

36. Most have observed the ways in which the theological perspective of the center criticizes the frame. Whedbee (1977:7) has observed that the reverse is true as well. The viewpoint from the

heavenly council demonstrates that the argument of the friends is wrongheaded.

37. Crenshaw (1981:100-105) discusses the literary importance of the prologue and epilogue.

38. Whedbee (1977:6) speaks of the two-fold purpose of this first tradent of the story: "[B]y cutting [the tale] . . . in two parts and making it into a prologue and epilogue . . . the genre and intention are thereby transformed . . . [the poet] has fractured the integrity of the original narrative and forced it to . . . [supply] the framework in which the poetic dialogues unfold, and at the same time provide the fundamental story line." Westermann (1981:8) suggests that the frame provided "the poem its character as an event [rather than an abstract philosophical discourse]." Kinet (1983:34) asserts that the poet used the frame "so he could then introduce more unobtrusively his daring attack on the God of classic orthodox theology.

39. Veronika Kubina (1979:115-123) argues for the literary unity of the speeches on the basis of vocabulary.

40. MacDonald (1895:70) says, "The speech of Elihu was more a criticism of the book than a criticism of Job."

41. Dhorme (1967:lxiv) probably overstates the case in saying "The monument which the author aims at creating is the poem. The Prologue and Epilogue are no more than its entrance and exit." Girard (1987:144) claims that the frame functions as "shock absorbers [making] possible the preservation of texts that no one reads, since they are meaningless within the context given them."

42. Not coincidentally, the efforts of the later tradent also serve to make the book less accessible to those in Israelite society who did not constitute the intellectual elite. Legendary Job belonged (as did most oral tales) to the tribal, less urbanized, less formally educated segments of society.

NOTES TO CHAPTER 3:
DISSONANCE AND POINTS OF ACCESS

1. The theoretical analysis in Chapter 1 is based on the assumption that the text is single and unitary. The unique history of Job compels a more complicated model allowing that parts of the text were written at separate historical moments.

2. For Spivak (1976:lxxxiv), the analysis consists of "The interweaving of different texts . . . in an act of criticism that refuses to think of 'influence' or 'interrelationship' as a simple historical phenomenon."

3. Greenberg (1987:301) offers: "The effect of keeping the background setting and the foreground dialogue simultaneously in the mind is almost vertiginous."

4. Of course, much of the simple piety of the frame narrative is in fact only on the surface. There is much sophisticated questioning of God found in the frame.

5. Crenshaw (1977b:63) notes that Job consists of "two acts running concurrently and performed on different stages."

6. As with the production of literature, so reading too is an exceedingly complex activity, involving both the highlighting of certain harmonious features that accord with the particular world-view (ideology) of the reader, and the suppression of many elements that threaten that ideology. The conflicts thus produced (because that which is suppressed is never truly eradicated) closely parallel the dissonance in textual production.

7. Vermeylan (1986:62-63) asserts that the author's sympathies are neither with the friends nor with Job, but rather the author caricatures both positions in order to reconcile them.

8. It is assumed of course that the center did not have an independent existence but depended upon the legendary story for inspiration and context. That dependence, however, took the form of a conflict, as the two artistic sensibilities (of the ancient tellers of the folk tale and the later, more intellectual poet) both struggled for control of the dominant symbols within the work. Legendary Job, although complex and ironic in its attacks on ancient notions of retribution, generated a single theological notion: a universe where God's moral governance was undiscernible to humankind, and where humans must continue to affirm (or at least not deny) the eternal verities. Likewise, the dialogues between Job and his friends, though incomplete without the frame, had a unitary notion as well: that human integrity demanded an honest attack on the wisdom of a god who allows such things to take place.

9. The different voices might be outlined as follows:
A. Folk Tale (frame)
    1. Denial of retribution and affirmation of faithful service.
    2. Implied affirmation of principle of retribution (it is assumed even though not operative.) It is affirmed by the cry of pain evoked by its absence.
    3. Implied deconstruction of pious behavior. (This was the inspiration for the center.)
B. The Center
    1. Denial of faithful service as well as hope.
    2. Implied affirmation of faithful service and hope.
    3. Implied nihilism.

10. His statements represent "the very formula of oriental resignation. The only course is to allow the sovereign Ruler of the world to act as He wills" (Dhorme 1967:13). Janzen (1985:31) describes these responses as, "those symbolic means by which one's world remains

hedged about when calamity strikes one physically and socially and materially." See also Vogels 1980:845.

11. Weiss (1983:69) sees in the silence, "a psychological defense against a rebellious outburst, preventing him from speaking out against God.

12. "The Talmud (Bab., Baba Batra 16b) presents the possibility, "with his lips he did not sin, but in his heart, he sinned," quoted in Weiss 1983:71.

13. It is not fair to equate all expressions of piety with social conservatism. Some particular expressions may actually threaten the social institutions. The question here raised is the relationship between piety and prosperity: Is Job rich because he is pious, or is he pious so that he may become rich? Although the topic in the center seems to change, it still concerns the "act-consequence nexus:" do people suffer because of sin? (Clines, 1985:133).

14. Cook (1968:12) notes "The standard form [of his pious confession] does not meet the tremendous demands of a situation he senses far within himself to transcend even such utterances of total acceptance."

15. Herbert Chanan Brichto (1968:217) identifies the concept of curse in Job as not imprecation but rather "to treat in a disrespectful manner . . . [to] repudiate."

16. Johannes Pedersen (1926:367) notes that this condition of inner righteousness is absolutely central to Israelite cultural values. "Where the righteousness of men and the justice of God clash, there is no way out, because life is based upon the complete harmony between the two" (368).

17. Note these other verses in Job that make reference to traditional pious notions: 4:6, "Is not your piety your confidence,/ Your integrity your hope?" 8:6, "If you are blameless and upright/ He [God] will protect you,/ And grant well-being to your righteous home."

18. Cook (1968:14-15) relates *tûmah* to *tam* "perfect," referring to "an unblemished wholeness that makes a sacrificial animal fit to be offered to God."

19. "'Integrity' is the repeated unifying expression for that in Job which constitutes his justification" (Cook:19).

20. Surprisingly, Moore (1983:27) has argued that Job loses his integrity through moral vacillation in his arguments. Job's death wish, says Moore (28) is incompatible with integrity. His argument lacks cogency, based as it is on pious standards alien to the text. Job's integrity shines clearly through the myriads of arguments and various positions defended and attacked. Bloch (1972:107) notes, "And it is Yahweh who is on the defensive, thrust back by the most powerful attacks on his righteousness."

21. Moore (1983:26) sees Job 3 as "a negative commentary upon the pious Job of the prologue" (see also 30-31). Crenshaw (1977b:65)

observes, "It therefore shocks the reader to note Job's capitulation to God in the epilogue. It constitutes Job's loss of integrity." Michael Fishbane (1971:53) describes Job 3 as "an absolute and unrestrained death wish for himself and the entire creation."

22. Polzin (1974:184) observes, "Within these . . . chapters of Job's speeches can be found examples of some of the most anti-Yahwist sentiments of which we have any record in literature." Many others say that he skirts the edges of blasphemy but never crosses over into unrestrained cursing (Good 1973:476; Whedbee 1977:8). Dhorme (1967:lxxxi-iii) believes he is free from any taint of blasphemy. "Rather he has spoken of things he was not aware."

23. Vawter (1983:51) translates 3:3, "Damn the day when I was born," a complaint lodged against the providence of Yahweh.

24. God uses "the sickness-causing demons as poison arrows and says that God is shooting them at him, so that his life is soaking up their venom," Job 6:4 (Robertson 1977:39). God is accused of immorality, Job 9:22-24 (Carroll 1975:162).

25. "What have I done to you, O watcher (policeman) of men?" (Van Selms 1985:1).

26. Terrien (1954:889) summarizes Job's accusations as follows: God is a capricious tyrant (9:18-19), a corrupt judge (9:20-29), a wild beast which has torn his flesh (16:7-9), a ruthless warrior (Job 6:4, 9; 16:12-14; 19:18-19).

27. Robertson (1977:45) asserts that Job wants to hire an avenger to murder God. See also, Westermann 1983:19.

28. Job exposes "the dark side of God as the beast, the hunter, and the spy" (Habel 1985:53).

29. One must of course note the "rhetorical brinksmanship" of the Joban poet (Moore 1983:24). Why does not this bold writer just come out and curse God, as is clearly his covert intention? One might speculate irrefutable societal taboos, or a practical effort to make his or her ideas palatable to a reading public; or perhaps the author, by avoiding this decisive final break with deity, endeavored to say something significant about Job, that he maintains some sense of religious affection. Many have speculated that the disrupted third cycle of speeches betrays a suppressed unambiguously blasphemous speech (Terrien 1954:888). For further discussion of curse in the Hebrew Bible with reference to Job, see Scharbert 1958:2, 16; Herbert and Snaith 1952:111; Blank 1950-1951:84; Harrelson 1962:447; Brichto 1968: 217-218.

30. Some of Job's speeches in the dialogues proclaim his unwavering faith in the midst of his more frequent insults hurled at Yahweh (Westermann 1983:21). There is no clearly discernible section of Job that presumes a single theological position.

31. Crenshaw (1987:376) speaking of the friends' defense of divine justice notes, "Like their heavenly counterparts, rulers were

thought to champion the cause of justice." Knierim (1973:438) states, "Through most of the history of civilization, the human institutions, and not only the cultic ones, were never thought of by their founders other than as earthly copies, images and materializations of the primordial world."

32. Terrien (1954:902), Day (198:86) and others have determined that the speeches depict a powerful and mysterious God who transcends human standards of good and evil. These readings fail to account for Yahweh's inadequate response to Job's dilemma.

33. There are various shifting theories of the purpose of the speeches of Yahweh. For some the theophany has value in and of itself, regardless of the content of Yahweh's words (Terrien 1954:902). For Day (1986:86), the argument shifts from an anthropocentric to a theocentric basis, elucidating the conflict between the personal God of Job and the cosmic God that the author of Job puts forth. God is thus freed from any moral requirements towards humanity. Finally, others say that God is herein depicted as an overpowering bully. R. A. F. MacKenzie (1959:436) describes Yahweh's rejoinder: "It is like waving a rattle before a crying infant, to distract him from hunger." C. G. Jung (1956:378) suggests, "it is Yahweh himself who darkens his own counsel."

34. Williams (1971:236) observes, "It very clearly may be understood as a condemnation of God—by God."

35. "Because he was not destroyed, he was vindicated" (Habel 1985:65).

36. Glatzer (1969:11) speaks of "the Jewish interpreters in the premodern period who Judaized Job and Christian expositors who Christianized him. Both sides . . . avoided a direct confrontation with the text of the book. . . By concentrating on the story of a patient, saintly Job, the reader could absorb the shock of the drama of the rebellious hero; he could interpret the latter in the light of the former." In an earlier text Glatzer remarks (1966:197), "Such latitude permitted remarkable freedom of interpretation and provoked the conception of a number of self-contained compositions in which Job appears as a symbolic representation of a particular attitude to God and the world."

37. Glatzer (1966) surveys the following "stories" read from Job, and traces them historically: "Job the Saint;" as in the New Testament Book of James, "Job the Imperfectly Pious man;" "Job the Rebel;" "Job the Dualist;" which is a polemic against a view that evil resides in a negative spiritual being who counters God's good influence, "Job the Pious Man in Search of an Answer;" wherein Job was not rebellious. He only wanted instruction and information; "Job the Man Lacking in True Knowledge,"—his sin was ignorance; and many others.

38. Implied readers are those one expects to be reading the work. It is assumedly something in the mind of the writer, but is more directly in the mind of the interpretive community. This implied reader could

either be circumscribed by the particular culture that produced the text, or else interpreted more broadly, including readers from wider geographic and chronological locations.

39. Many contend that Job in fact does not repent and abase himself, but rather strikes back in a last futile act of rebellion. This may be seen as an alternative construction of the story of rebellious Job.

40. That is, the text seen as the dissonant confluence of readings. Kubina (1979:70ff) suggests that the final form of Job reflects the world of the Egyptian Jewish community, based on various thematic and mythological similarities.

41. The vagueness of references to those Israelite groups indicates the speculative character of such historical reconstructions. Although most critics date the final edition of Job to the post-exilic era, no contemporary writer in post-exilic history that I am aware of has used the text of Job to provide information about the history of that period. This indicates the tenuous nature of this connection.

42. "'Blameless' refers to his character, 'upright' refers to his actions" (Weiss 1983:25); "'Blameless' . . . means 'whole, complete, integral . . . '; 'upright' . . . means . . . straight as opposed to 'crooked'" (Robertson 1977:34).

43. "The Sons of the East, people mythically wise, speaks both of Job's superlative wisdom, but also the honor he received from the sages" (Weiss 1983:27). Yahweh actually widens the compliment, declaring Job as the greatest on the earth.

44. Three other readings of Yahweh's speeches, surveyed by Tsevat (1966:93-95) are: (1) "education through overwhelming . . . Job is reduced to submission"; (2) "God teaches Job that divine justice . . . is greater than human justice"; (3) "The beauty of nature is an 'anodyne' to human suffering."

45. Good (1973:481) states that Job repents "for his being satisfied to know all about God at secondhand, and for elevating himself to deity's rank." Others see the entire text of Job's response as hopelessly damaged, resisting reliable interpretation (Westermann 1981:125). Rowley (1970:20) feels that Job repented of the foolish things he said in the prologue. Vermeylen (1986:54-55) provides a complete survey of the positions.

46. John Briggs Curtis (1979:507, 510) reads the statements (40:4, 42:6) as a complete and violent rejection of God: "I will now with contemptuous revulsion cease speaking altogether . . . Therefore I feel loathing contempt and revulsion/(toward you, O God);/ and I am sorry for frail man." Jung (1956:318) sees Job's "ultimate realization that might, not right is the crux of the issue." Robertson (1977:52) states that Job's confession is insincere, tongue in cheek in order to calm God's whirlwind.

47. What this line may have meant in a different, more original context is not germane to the present discussion. Batten (1933:126)

comments on Job 42:7, "The striking feature in this section is the commendation of Job, and that not for his endurance of misery as in 2:3, but for what he had said. Further, the words for which he is praised are not those of submission to Jahveh . . . but for those uttered in the discussion with Eliphaz, Bildad and Zophar."

48. Moore (1983:21) observes, "In agreement with a divine rebuke, Job says 'I have been wrong,' whereupon God says 'You have been right." Snaith (1968:4) notes, "If any man has transgressed the limits of what is proper to say about God, it is Job." "Job is being praised for having berated the Lord, challenged him, satirized him, dared him, spurned him" (Vawter 1983:85). "If what Job had to say also agreed with what God had to say then it seems rather unfair that Job should be indicted with the question 'Who is this that darkens counsel by words without knowledge?'" (Carroll 1975:162). "Once the present dialogues were substituted for the originals, however, God's praise of Job amounts to a terrible self-incrimination . . . God is the object of an ironic joke" (Robertson 1977:53).

49. "[It does not seem] likely that it should be a commendation of his final capitulation in 42:1-6 for that would make the contrast with what his friends had to say pointless. But if the statement is allowed to carry maximal content then it opens up a wide range of reference" (Carroll 1975:161).

50. "For Job whose eyes had dwelt on the past there can have been no thorough restoration but a terrible sense of loss and perhaps even impotent rage against a power that had so casually discarded his life to settle a wager" (Carroll 1975:164). Of course, few commentators, when reflecting on Job's misery, acknowledge the personal fate of the children and servants who represent not only a loss to Job, but a more serious loss to themselves (Crenshaw 1984:57).

51. Duquoc (1983:84) sees in Yahweh's approbation "God's recognition of the right to revolt." "[He] is more honored by the impatience and revolt of Job than by the adulation of the 'friends' who recognize the designs of providence where God himself says he sees no such thing" (86).

52. "His task being not to tempt man to evil but to spot evil men. Likewise the Satan is not the enemy of God; rather he is God's servant. But in this case it does seem that a kind of rivalry has sprung up between them" (Robertson 1977:35). Snaith (1968:2) points out, "Already by the time the prologue of the book of Job was written, the Satan has become more than a little cynical, so that when God declares that Job is perfect and upright, the Satan takes leave to cast doubts."

53. Jung (1956:375) writes, "It is indeed no edifying spectacle to see how quickly Yahweh abandons his faithful servant to the evil spirit and lets him fall without compunction or pity into the abyss of physical and moral suffering."

54. Terrien (1954:912-913) describes the Satanic attitude as "impudence."

55. Weiss (1983:67) has an interesting observation on 2:7: "The reader, who knows what Job does not, will understand what the sentence means, namely, that the subject of 'smote' is the subject of the previous sentence: Satan. To Job, who does not know what the reader knows, the subject of the sentence is the object of the previous clause: the Lord."

56. Day (1986:67-68) makes a convincing case for an ironic use of the mediator theme in the Joban dialogues. Job looks for a heavenly advocate to plead his case, but the only heavenly presence appears before God as Job's enemy.

57. Later than the period of legendary Job, whose shapers would assumedly not be too squeamish to depict the deity in compromising positions.

58. The scenes of the Heavenly Council were a crucial element in the original story and probably no Satan figure.

59. Dhorme (1967:xxix) identifies the divine fire as "the instrument of divine vengeance."

60. It is conceivable that these would be dead cliches devoid of meaning or significance, but in such a tight narrative of carefully chosen words this is unlikely. Tur-Sinai (1967:31) notes in 1 Kings 18:38 and 2 Kings 1:10 that this is divine activity.

61. Clines (1985:129-130) observes (overstating the case): "The absence of a sixth scene of Yahweh's vindication over Satan . . . is of course of the essence of the book."

62. Weiss (1983:37) treats the Satan as a hypostatization of God's darker side, God's negative untrusting aspects, so God himself remains pure. "The storyteller sought to preclude the notion that He who is all knowing can have any doubt (39). So also Vawter 1983:30, 39.

63. This same word described Job's relationship to Yahweh. Satan accused Job of not serving God without "expectation of reward" (*hinnam*), which accusation was proved false in the prologue. Yahweh seems to indicate that the test, having taken place, was "pointless," not worth the suffering caused to Job. One can not help but be amazed therefore when Yahweh consents to an even more traumatic test. Although Yahweh admits to afflicting Job "needlessly" (*hinnam*) he clearly does not love Job "in a gratuitous manner" *hinnam*, but requires ever deeper and more costly proof. By use of the same word in both contexts, Job's piety is contrasted with God's love. Yahweh is again minimized by the context. (Quotation marks indicate some of the semantic diversity of this word.) For discussions on the use of this word, see Weiss 1983:65; 82; Driver 1921:21; Dhorme 1967:lxxxiv.

64. Clines (1985:130) disagrees, claiming that God is the only initiator of the action. He confuses the formal relationship between

Yahweh and Satan with the actual lines of force that run between them. So also Sarna 1957:23.

65. Robertson (1977:54) has suggested that the author deliberately ridicules Yahweh so as to make him less a fearsome object. Habel (1983:108) notes, "God's pride so blinded Him that he was vulnerable to the enticement of Satan. Though he is conscious of his first entice-ment, God falls prey to Satan's wager a second time . . . Nowhere does God ever express any emotional feelings of concern for Job."

66. Concerning the absence of Satan, Robertson (1977:36) observes, "We expect to be returned to heaven and listen to God claim his victory. But instead we hear that three friends of Job have come to console him. Nothing so far has hinted that anything like this would happen. It breaks the close construction of the plot and so prepares for some intensification of the drama."

67. Good (1973:475) takes exception to the use of the term wager, by seeing the Satan's formula as a solemn curse rather than a frivolous bet. But rather than eliminate the concept of a wager, Good has merely pointed out how high Satan had placed the stakes.

68. Even the question of disinterested piety, seemingly answered in the prologue, is questioned in the center where Job acts anything but disinterested.

69. A privileged reading is one that is sanctioned by a particular culture as the "correct" one.

NOTES TO CHAPTER 4:
THE BOOK OF JOB IN THE WORLD

1. Biblical books that in part attacked the Deuteronomistic impulse would include Jeremiah, Habakkuk, Job, Qoheleth, Jonah. According to Vermeylan (1986:57-59) the arguments of the friends represent another post-exilic group who defended Yahweh's faithfulness rather than vocalizations of traditional pre-exilic Yahwistic orthodoxy.

2. Strictly speaking, there is no absolutely final redaction, but there is a general period where the text became substantially fixed.

3. A conflict remains within the discussion of wisdom in Israel. I follow Gerhard von Rad (1972:15-23) and Crenshaw (1981:27-31) who affirm a distinct group of sages who taught in Israel, a class of intelligentsia, theoreticians who educated the extended royal family and participated in court politics. Others (Whybray 1974) insist that sapiential influence pervaded all levels and groups in Israelite society and never developed the cluster of special interests and terminology that would constitute a separable group.

4. Communities enforce readings in many ways, but primarily through control of the major interpretive institutions. Enforced read-

ings are maintained in much the same way in the modern era. See my discussion of "Society and Author," Chapter 1.

5. There is no intrinsic reason to privilege *older* readings of texts over newer readings.

6. Jameson (1981:81) proposes this type of interpretation: "The rewriting of the literary text in such a way that the latter may itself be seen as the rewriting or restructuration of a prior historical or ideological *subtext* . . . [which] must itself always be (re)constructed after the fact."

7. This understanding of God is distinguished from the "cynical reading," which offers a definitive, though negative, view of God. The dissonantal reading of God endeavors to resist *any* notion of definitiveness. It remains cloudy. Even God's absence is obscured.

8. Robertson (1977:45) contends that this redeemer was hired to murder God.

9. Gordis (1965:71) states, "For the ancient Hebrews, who could not conceive of God's existence apart from His governing the world, to attribute evil to any other power beyond His sway would be tantamount to a denial of God."

10. McFague (1987:xi) (among others) has called for a "remythologization" of God along lines that are more appropriate for the modern era. "Much *deconstruction* of the traditional imagery has taken place, but little *construction*" (ibid). "Rather, theology must be self-conscuously constructive, willing to think differently from the past" (ibid, p. 21).

11. Margarete Susman (1969:92) observes, "The process against God must assume a new shape; it must start anew and in a new vision: a version in which God is all silence and man alone speaks."

12. Lou Silberman (1985:6, 9, 10) observes "All that is to be said of Deity is inappropriate . . . That, on a preliminary level, is what is intended by metaphor . . . If this then is the case, the Hebrew Bible, or large parts of it, is a vast, intricate, many leveled network of metaphors, personal pronouns, that at once conceals and reveals Deity."

13. "For to create a metaphor is to impose a limit whilst this metaphor in denying limits paradoxically denies metaphoricity" (Silberman 1985:34).

14. McFague (1987:64) criticizes this concept for the following reasons: "In this picture God can be God only if we are nothing . . . The relationship of a king to his subjects is necessarily a distant one: royalty is 'untouchable.' It is the distance, the difference, the otherness of God that is underscored with this image." One must of course distinguish the monarchic metaphor for God from Silberman's unmetaphoricity. Although both stress the transcendence of deity, the traditional configurations describe this transcendence in terms of various hierarchical human social systems.

15. "A new imaginative picture of the relationship between God and the world must precede action" (McFague 1987:xiv).

16. McFague (1987:98-99) states, "[First] God should be imagined in female, not feminine, terms, and second, the female metaphors should be inclusive of but not limited to maternal ones. On the first point: the distinction between 'female' and 'feminine' is important, for the first refers to gender while the second refers to qualities conventionally associated with women. The problem invariably ends with identifying as female those qualities that society has called feminine. Thus the feminine side of God is taken to comprise the tender, nurturing, passive, healing aspects of divine activity."

16. Raschke (1982:28) states "Deconstruction, therefore, can be seen as a kind of Bacchic fascination with the metaphysics of decomposition and death . . . it serves as a simile for the return of the repressed feminine in a predominantly patriarchal academy." He goes on to quote Derrida: "Woman is one name for this nontruth of truth."

17. I am indebted to McFague's discussion of the world as God's body (1987:59-87).

18. Thought of as empty vestiges from a previous mythological point of view on the part of Israel's forebears. It is doubtful, however, that the mythological material employed by Job and other poetic works was totally defused. Rather they represented the persistent mythological impulse always there under the surface in Israel's religious conceptualization. Fishbane (1971:159) notes that these mythological references are "cultural deposits and subsurface images."

19. Bloch (1972:110) "A man has overtaken, has enlightened his own God. That, despite the apparent submission at the end, is the abiding lesson of the book of Job."

20. See Vermeylen (1986:21) for a discussion of Job's hope.

21. Crenshaw (1984:117) refers to Job and others: "The astonishing thing about every single one of these instances of divine testing is a stubborn refusal to abandon God, despite the fact that to do so would bring blessed relief."

22. Job never ceases to be a "rich" man in his sensibilities, in his expectation as to the way the world should be, and in his attitudes towards his contemporaries, his "inferiors." "But now those younger than I deride me,/ [Men] whose fathers I would have disdained to put among my sheep dogs," Job 30:1. See also 19:9-18, 11:89-90. Girard (1987:12) compares Job to the tyrant of the Greek cities. Crenshaw (1984:72) asserts that in Job 19:19 "Job is portrayed as a king who has been removed from his throne . . . Not only does he threaten to approach God like a prince, but he also describes his status in the gates as that of a king among subjects."

23. This term is defined as one who can serve as a pattern for other individuals. He may serve a generalized function in others' self-identity. There is an ease in recontextualizing him in different cultural

situations. As Crenshaw (1977b:67) says, "We read about Job and see ourselves in the hero, or the villain. We lack the power to remain untouched by the profundity of the drama."

24. I am aware of an enormous body of literature known as "holocaust studies," with which I am not conversant. The following is meant to be suggestive rather than programmatic. Information concerning the holocaust is an entire field in itself that must be mastered to carry this sort of work to completion.

25. "I asked Alfred Kazin one day if he thought the death of six million Jews could have any meaning; and he replied that he hoped not. There can, indeed, be no answer naked enough, or real enough" (Wiesel, 1982:162)·

26. Susman (1969:92) notes, "The revealed God whom the Jew has accepted has become in a manner unimaginable till now, the Deus absconditus, the absent God, the God who simply can no longer be found."

27. There is ample historical documentation that individuals and nations that could have saved many (if not most) of the concentration camp victims declined to do so. By way of comparison, I note Crenshaw (1984:71) who comments, "The very fact that no one came to Job's defense spoke volumes about the persons in authority." Girard (1987) has made this theme, so prominent in the dialogues, his primary interpretive key.

28. McFague attempts such myth creation in her book, Models of God (1987).

29. Susman (1969:92) states, "The Jew cannot remain silent when God hides Himself now as he hid Himself before Job because just as He evaded Job in his personal fate so He evades the modern Jew in his universal fate."

30. Crenshaw (1987:375) notes, "Divine perfidy and human suffering ought to evoke a loud outcry that can be heard above Job's enforced silence."

31. Crenshaw (1987:378) comments, "The inadequacy of this view . . . has not hastened its demise."

32. Crenshaw (1987:378) observes, "Hope became temporarily and spatially separated from existence on this earth . . . In the next life wrongs would be rectified, for every hidden thing would be exposed to the light of day."

NOTES TO APPENDIX:
THE DATING OF JOB

1. Vermeylan (1986:57-59, 61-62) notes important similarities between the Psalms of lament and the book of Job.

2. Van Selm's assertion of the universal nature of Job rather begs the question, but the attack on "developmental dating" is well taken.

3. Vermeylan (1986:65) stands almost alone in seeing Job's perfection as a later addition.

4. Robert H. Pfeiffer (1926:13) identifies Edomitic wisdom with the opposition to the law of retribution found in the book of Job.

5. She also notes the similarities between the activity of the Satan and the Babylonian sickness demons (82). See the Babylonian poem, "I Will Praise the Lord of Wisdom" (Pritchard 1969:435). See also Sarna (1957:23), Whedbee (1977:7-8) who calls it "an age-old mythical motif," and Terrien (1954:879) who characterizes the account as possessing "an undeniably . . . polytheistic flavor."

6. Day (1986:161) sees an individual Satan, as opposed to an anonymous member of the heavenly court as characteristically late. She sees the Satan of Job as a key feature of the poet's work in the center (68-75) and notes that *hassatan* may mean "a certain adversary from among the *bene ha'elohim*" (43). Pope (1973:10) suggests that the concept came from the Persian secret service, where a spy was described as the "eyes and ears of the king."

7. Unusual features in the frame that might conform more fully to a late dating are offered to prove this assertion. There are two bases for this argument. The first is grammatical, that the ambiguous subject in 1:13 ("his sons") requires a clear antecedent, supplied by verse 5. Therefore verses 6-12 (the first heavenly scene) are considered later additions. The second reason is theological, the picture of Satan being more consistent with a late Persian theology (Hurvitz 1974:18).

8. This is comparable, he says, to the transference of responsibility from Yahweh to Satan in the tempting of David reported in 2 Samuel 24 (early) and 1 Chronicles 22 (late). See Day (1986:113-132) for a dissenting position.

9. He contends that Israelites only questioned the morality of their God late in their history. Crenshaw (1980:9-10) observes two sources for skepticism in Israel. The first (theological), must be supplemented by a fundamental epistemological doubt that cannot be limited to a particular historical situation.

10. Hans-Peter Müller (1978:49-72) surveys the parallel texts from the ancient Near East.

11. He refers to a Hebrew article by Cassuto where he notes that Hebrew prose (so-called) is often an extension of the Canaanite epic tradition (18). Snaith (1968:21-27) contends that the "Babylonian Job" corresponds to "the first edition" of Job, a skeletal form of the frame as it now exists. Snaith (21) develops a fascinating but ultimately not compelling thesis that the prose-dialogue-prose form of Job reflects an ancient form found in many ANE texts. He thereby asserts that the book was created in substantially the same form in which it now exists (minus Elihu). I am not convinced, the problem not being due to the prose-dialogue-prose form, but to the significant stylistic and theologi-

cal dissonance between the parts which cannot be accounted for by any ANE pattern.

12. MacDonald (1898:38) notes: "If the reference here is to the Job of our book . . . Ezekiel must have been hard driven for cases in point."

13. He also surveys discussion of Job in the early Church fathers and in early Islamic writers that reflect a faithful and patient Job, rather than the more philosophical questioning Job of the canonical text (140-141). See also Müller 1978:26-30. Nahum N. Glatzer (1969: 15) reports: "Bishop Theodore of Mopsuestia (died 428) . . . accepted this popular story of Job as the true account, dismissing the biblical book of Job as a mere literary product written by a man anxious to parade his learning and to gain repute." "Early Talmudic-midrashic literature treats Job as the most pious Gentile that ever lived" (17). In following pages he surveys both Jewish and Christian interpreters who support the view of Job as pious, reflecting the legendary tale.

BIBLIOGRAPHY

Ackroyd, Peter. R. 1968. *Exile and Restoration*. Philadelphia: Westminster.

Batten, L. W. 1933. "The Epilogue in the Book of Job." *Anglican Theological Review* 15:125-128.

Blackmur, R. P. 1971. "A Critic's Job of Work." Pp. 891-904 in *Critical Theory Since Plato*. Hazard Adams, ed. New York: Harcourt, Brace & Jovanovich.

Blank, Sheldon H. 1950-1951. "The Curse, The Blasphemy, The Spell, The Oath." *Hebrew Union College Annual* 23:73-95.

Bloch, Ernst. 1972. *Atheism and Christianity*. J. T. Swann, trans. New York: Herder & Herder.

Brichto, Herbert Chanan. 1960. *The Problem of "Curse" in the Hebrew Bible*. Philadelphia: SBL.

Brown, Frank Burch. 1982. "Transfiguration: Poetic Metaphor and Theological Reflection." *Journal of Religion* 62:39-56.

Buechner, Frederick. 1987. *Brendan*. New York: Atheneum.

Carroll, R. P. 1975. "Postscript on Job." *The Modern Churchman* 18: 161-166.

Clines, D. J. A. 1985. "False Naivety in the Prologue to Job." *Hebrew Union Annual Review* 9:127-136.

Cook, Albert. 1968. *The Root of the Thing: A Study of Job and the Song of Songs*. Bloomington: Indiana Univ.

Crenshaw, James L. 1980. "The Birth of Skepticism in Ancient Israel" Pp. 1-19 in *The Divine Helmsman*. James L. Crenshaw & Samuel Sandmal, eds. New York: Ktav.

————. 1977a. "In Search of Divine Presence." *Review and Expositor* 74: 353-369.

————. 1977b. "The Two-Fold Search: A Response to Louis Alonso Schockel." *Semeia* 7:63-69.

————. 1981. *Old Testament Wisdom: An Introduction*. Atlanta: John Knox.

————. 1984. *Whirlpool of Torment*. Philadelphia: Fortress.

————. 1987. "The High Cost of Preserving God's Honor." *The World and I*. 2:375-382.

Culler, Jonathan. 1972. "Language and Knowledge." *The Yale Review* 62:290-296.

Curtis, John Briggs. 1979. "On Job's Response to Yahweh." *JBL* 98: 497-511.

Dahood, Mitchell. 1966. *Psalms I*. Garden City: Doubleday.

Day, Peggy Lynne. 1986. *"Satan" In the Hebrew Bible*. Ph.D. Diss., Harvard Univ.

Derrida, Jacques. 1976. *On Grammatology*. With a preface by Gayatri Chakravorty Spivak. Baltimore: John Hopkins Univ.

De Wilde, A. 1981. *Das Buch Hiob*. Leiden: E. J. Brill.

Dhorme E. 1967. *A Commentary on the Book of Job*. Harold Knight, trans. London: Thomas Nelson.

Driver, Samuel Rolles & George Bray Buchanan. 1921. *A Critical and Exegetical Commentary on the Book of Job*. Edinburgh: Clark.

Duquoc, Christian. 1983. "Demonism and the Unexpectedness of God. Pp. 81-87 in *Job and the Silence of God*. Christian Duquoc & Casiano Floristan, eds. Edinburgh: Clark.

Eagleton, Terry. 1983. *Literary Theory: An Introduction*. Oxford: Blackwell.

Erickson, John D. 1983. "Review of *The Political Unconscious*." *French Review* 56:626-628.

Ferguson, Frances C. 1974. "The Politics of Language. *Partisan Review* 41:310-314.

Fishbane, Michael. 1971. "Jeremiah IV 23-26 and Job II 3-13: A Recovered Use of the Creation Pattern." *VT* 21:151-167.

Fohrer, Georg. 1983. *Studien zum Buche Hiob*. Berlin: de Gruyter.

Foucault, Michel. 1984. "What is an Author?" Pp. 101-102 in *The Foucault Reader* Paul Rabinowitz, ed. New York: Pantheon Books.

Funt, David Paul. 1973. "Review of *The Prison-House of Language*." *Hudson Review* 26:410-414.

Fullerton, Kember. 1924. "The Original Conclusion to the Book of Job." *ZAW* 42:116-135.

Gehman, Henry S. 1949. "The Theological Approach of the Greek Translator of Job 1-15." *JBL* 68:231-240.

Girard, René. 1987. *Job, The Victim of His People*. Yvonne Freccero, trans. Stanford: Stanford Univ.

Glatzer, Nahum N. 1966. "The Book of Job and Its Interpreters." Pp. 197-220 in *Biblical Motifs*. Alexander Altmann, ed. Cambridge: Harvard Univ.

———. 1969. "Introduction: A Study of Job." Pp. 1-48 in *The Dimensions of Job*. New York: Schocken Books.

Good, Edwin M. 1973. "Job and the Literary Task: A Response." *Soundings* 56:470-484.

Gordis, Robert. 1965. *The Book of God and Man: A Study of Job*. Chicago: Univ. of Chicago.

Greenberg, Moshe. 1987. "Job." Pp. 283-304 in *The Literary Guide to the Bible*. Robert Alter & Frank Kermode, eds. Cambridge: Harvard Univ.

Haag, Herbert. 1974. *Teufelglaube*. Tübingen: Katzman.

Habel, Norman. 1983. "The Narrative Art of Job." *JSOT* 27:101-111.

———. 1985. *The Book of Job: A Commentary*. Philadelphia: Westminster.

Harrelson, Walter J. 1962. "Blessings and Cursings." Pp. 446-448 in *Interpreter's Dictionary of the Bible*, Vol. 1. George Arthur Buttrick, ed. Nashville: Abingdon.

Herbert, A. G. & Snaith, N. H. 1952. "A Study of the Words 'Curse and 'Righteousness.'" *The Bible Translator* 3:111-114.

Hoffman, Yair. 1981. "The Relationship Between the Prologue and the Speech-Cycles of Job: A Reconsideration." *VT* 31:160-170.

Hurvitz, Avi. 1974. "The Date of the Prose-Tale of Job Linguistically Reconsidered." *Harvard Theological Review* 67:17-34.

Jameson, Fredric. 1971. *Marxism and Form*. Princeton: Princeton Univ.

──────. 1972. *The Prison House of Language: A Critical Account of Structuralism and Russian Formalism.* Princeton: Princeton Univ.

──────. 1981. *The Political Unconscious: Narrative as a Socially Symbolic Act.* Ithaca: Cornell Univ.

Janzen, J. Gerald. 1985. *Job.* Atlanta: John Knox.

Jewish Publication Society. 1985. *Tanakh: A New Translation of the Holy Scripture.* Philadelphia: Jewish Publication Society.

Jung, C. G. 1956. "Answer to Job." Pp. 355-640 in *Psychology and Religion: West and East,* 2nd edn. R. F. C. Hull, trans. Princeton: Princeton Univ.

Kautzsch, Karl. 1900. *Das Sogenannte Volksbuch von Hiob.* Tübingen: Mohr.

Kinet, Dirk. 1983. "The Ambiguity of the Concepts of God and Satan in the Book of Job." Pp. 30-35 in *Job and the Silence of God.* Christian Duquoq & Casiano Floristano, eds. Edinburgh: Clark.

Kluger, Rivkah Scharf. 1967. *Satan in the Old Testament.* Hildegard Nagel, trans. Evanston: Northwestern Univ.

Knierim, Rolf. 1973. "Old Testament Form Criticism Reconsidered." *Interpretation* 27:435-468.

Koch, Klaus. 1983. "Is There a Doctrine of Retribution in the Old Testament?" Pp. 57-87 in *Theodicy in the Old Testament.* James L. Crenshaw, ed. Philadelphia: Fortress.

Kubina, Veronika. 1979. *Die Gottesreden im Buche Hiob.* Freiburg: Herder.

Lang, Bernhard. 1975. *Frau Weisheit.* Düsseldorf: Patmos.

Lentricchia, Frank. 1980. *After the New Criticism.* Chicago: Univ. of Chicago.

Lévêque, Jean. 1981. "Le Datation de Livre de Job." *Congress Volume* 32:206-219.

Lévi-Strauss, Claude. 1976. *Structural Anthropology,* Vol. 2. Monique Layton, trans. Chicago: Univ. of Chicago.

MacDonald, Duncan B. 1895. "The Original Form of the Legend of Job." *JBL* 14:63-67.

──────. 1898. "Some External Evidence of the Original Form of the Legend of Job." *The American Journal of Semitic Languages and Literatures* 14:138.

Macherey, Pierre. 1978. *A Theory of Literary Production.* Geoffrey Wall, trans. London: Routledge & Kegan Paul.

MacKenzie, R. A. F. 1959. "The Purpose of the Yahweh Speeches in the Book of Job. *Biblica* 40:435-445.

McFague, Sallie. 1987. *Models of God: Theology for an Ecological, Nuclear Age.* Philadelphia: Fortress.

Mitchell, Stephen. 1987. "The Book of Job." *The World and I* 2:346-367.

Moore, Rick D. 1983. "The Integrity of Job." *CBQ* 45:17-31.

Morgan, Donn F. 1981. *Wisdom in the Old Testament Tradition.* Atlanta: John Knox.

Müller, Hans-Peter. 1970. *Hiob und Seine Freunde.* Zurich: EVZ.

──────. 1978. *Das Hiobproblem.* Darmstadt: Wissenschaftlich Buchgesellschaft.

Murray, Gilbert. 1969. "Beyond Good and Evil." Pp. 194-197 in *Dimensions of Job.* Nahum Glatzer, ed. New York: Schocken.

Patrick, Dale. 1979. "Job's Address of God." *ZAW* 91:268-282.

Pedersen, Johannes. 1926. *Israel: Its Life and Culture*, Vols. 1-2. London: Oxford Univ.

Pfeiffer, Robert H. 1926. "Edomitic Wisdom." *ZAW* 44:13-25

Polzin, Robert M. 1977. *Biblical Structuralism: Method and Subjectivity in the Study of Ancient Texts*. Philadelphia: Fortress.

———. 1974."The Framework of the Book of Job." *Interpretation* 28:182-200.

Pope, Marvin H. 1973. *Job: Introduction, Translation and Notes*. Garden City: Doubleday.

Pritchard, James B., ed. 1969. *Texts Relating to the Old Testament*. Princeton: Princeton Univ.

Raschke, Carl A. 1982. "The Deconstruction of God." Pp. 1-33 in *Deconstruction and Theology*. Carl A. Raschke, ed. New York: Crossroads.

Roberts, J. J. M. 1977. "Job and the Israelite Religious Tradition." *ZAW* 89:107-114.

Robertson, David. 1977. *The Old Testament and the Literary Critic*. Philadelphia: Fortress.

Rowley, H. H. 1970. *Job*. London: Thomas Nelson.

Sarna, Nahum M. 1957. "Epic Substratum in the Prose of Job." *JBL* 76:13-25.

Scharbert, J. 1958. "'Fluchen' und 'Segnen' im Alten Testament." *Biblica* 39:1-26.

Scharlemann, Robert P. 1982. "The Being of God When God is Not Being God." Pp. 79-108 in *Deconstruction and Theology*. Carl A. Raschke, ed. New York: Crossroads.

Schmidt, Ludwig. 1976. *De Deo*. Berlin: Walter de Gruyter.

Scholes, Robert. 1984. "Review Essay: Interpretation and Narrative: Kermode and Jameson." *Novel: A Forum of Fiction* 17:270-271.

Seller, A. 1972."Language and Knowledge." *The Yale Review* 62:294.

Silberman, Lou. 1985. "Metaphors of Faith." Paper presented at the 1985 Cole Lectureship Series, Vanderbilt Univ.

Smith, Jonathan Z. 1983. "Wisdom and Apocalyptic." Pp.101-120 in *Visionaries and Their Apocalypses*. Paul D. Hanson, ed. Philadelphia: Fortress.

Snaith, Norman H. 1968. *The Book of Job: Its Origin and Purpose*. Naperville: Alen R. Allenson.

Spiegel, Shalom. 1945. "Noah, Danel and Job." Pp. 305-355 in *Louis Ginzberg Jubilee Volume*. New York: Ktav.

Spittler, R.P., trans. 1983. "The Testament Of Job." In *The Old Testament Pseudopigraphia*, Vol. 1. James H. Charlesworth, ed. New York: Doubleday.

Spivak, Gayatri Chakravorty. 1976. Preface to *Of Grammatology* by Jacques Derrida. Pp. ix-lxxxvii. Baltimore: Johns Hopkins Univ.

Sternberg, Meir. 1987. *The Poetics of Biblical Narrative: Ideological Literature and the Drama of Reading*. Bloomington: Indiana Univ.

Stevenson, William Barron. 1947. *The Poem of Job*. London: British Acad.

Stone, Michael E. 1983. "New Light on the Third Century." Pp. 85-96 in *Visionaries and Their Apocalypses*. Paul D. Hanson, ed. Philadelphia: Fortress.

Susman, Margarete. 1969. "God the Creator." Pp. 86-92 in *Dimensions of Job*. Nahum H. Gatzer, ed. New York: Schocken.

Taylor, Mark C. 1969. "The Text as Victim." Pp. 58-78 in *Dimensions of Job*. Nahum N. Gatzer, ed. New York: Schocken Books.

Terrien, Samuel. 1954."The Book of Job: Introduction and Exegesis." Pp. 877-1198 in *The Interpreter's Bible*, Vol. 3. George Arthur Buttrick, ed. New York: Abingdon.

Tsevat, Matitiahu. 1966. "The Meaning of the Book of Job." *Hebrew Union College Annual* 37:73-106.

Tur-Sinai, N. H. 1967. *The Book of Job: A New Commentary*. Jerusalem: Kiryath Sepher.

Van Selm, A. 1985. *Job: A Practical Commentary*. John Vriend, trans. Grand Rapids: William B. Eerdmans.

Vawter, Bruce. 1983. *Job and Jonah: Questioning the Hidden God*. New York: Paulist.

Vermeylen, J. 1986. *Job, Ses Amis et Son Dieu*. Leiden: E.J. Brill.

Vogels, Walter. 1980. "Job a Parlé Correctement." *Nouvelle Revu Théologique* 102:835-852.

von Rad, Gerhard. 1972. *Wisdom in Israel*. James D. Martin, trans. Nashville: Abingdon.

Weimann, Robert. 1969. "Past Significance and Present Meaning in Literary History." *New Literary History* 1:91-109.

Weiss, Meir. 1983. *The Story of Job's Beginnings*. Jerusalem: Magnes.

Weiss, Paul. 1969. "God, Job and Evil." Pp. 181-193 in *Dimensions of Job*. Nahum N. Glatzer, ed. New York: Schocken.

Westermann, Claus. 1981. *The Structure of the Book of Job: A Form Critical Analysis*. Charles A. Muenchow, trans. Philadelphia: Fortress.

———. 1983. "The Two Faces of Job." Pp. 15-22 in *Job and the Silence of God*. Christian Duquoc & Casiano Floristan, eds. Edinburgh: Clark.

Whedbee, William. 1977. "The Comedy of Job." *Semeia*. 1-40.

Wheelwright, Philip. 1962. *Metaphor and Reality*. Bloomington: Indiana Univ.

Whybray, R. N. 1974. *The Intellectual Tradition in the Old Testament*. Berlin & New York: de Gruyter.

Wiesel, Elie. 1960. *Night*. Stella Rodway, trans. New York: Avon.

———. 1982. *Legends of Our Time*. New York: Schocken.

Williams, James G. 1971. "You Have Not Spoken Truth of Me: Mystery and Irony in Job." *ZAW* 83:231-255.

Winquist, Charles E. 1982. "Body, Text, and Imagination." Pp. 34-57 in *Deconstruction and Theology*. Carl A. Raschke, ed. New York: Crossroad.

Zelnick, Stephen. 1979. "Review of *A Theory of Literary Production* by Pierre Macherey." *Journal of Aesthetics and Art Criticism* 38:213-215.

CBQ = *Catholic Biblical Quarterly*
JBL = *Journal of Biblical Literature*
JSOT = *Journal for the Study of the Old Testament*
VT = *Vetus Testamentum*
ZAW = *Zeitschrift für die Alttestamentliche Wissenschaft*

INDEXES

AUTHORS

SUBJECTS